SHAME
TRAVELS

Also by Jasvinder Sanghera:

Shame
Daughters of Shame

JASVINDER SANGHERA

SHAME TRAVELS

HODDER

First published in Great Britain in 2011 by Hodder & Stoughton
An Hachette UK company

First published in paperback in 2012

3

A CIP catalogue record for this title is available from the British Library

Paperback ISBN 978 0 340 96209 1

Typeset in Sabon by Hewer Text UK Ltd, Edinburgh

Printed and bound in the UK by CPI Group (UK) Ltd, Croydon, CR0 4YY

Hodder & Stoughton policy is to use papers that are natural,
renewable and recyclable products and made from wood grown in
sustainable forests. The logging and manufacturing processes are expected
to conform to the environmental regulations of the country of origin.

Hodder & Stoughton Ltd
338 Euston Road
London NW1 3BH

www.hodder.co.uk

For Natasha, Anna, Ben and Jordan;
and for Bachanu, a sister lost but now found forever

I have forsaken my house,
I have abandoned my heritage;
I have given the beloved of my soul
into the hands of her enemies.
My heritage has become to me
Like a lion in the forest,
She has lifted up her voice against
me;
Therefore I hate her.

Jeremiah xii, 7–8

AUTHOR'S NOTE

In my first book *Shame*, and the sequel *Daughters of Shame*, I gave my three children pseudonyms. But as I made the journey that forms the core of this book and wrote about it afterwards, I kept feeling that it was for them. It was our joint heritage that I went looking for, and what I found is a legacy for them as well as me. So this time round, with their permission, I've given them their real names: Natasha, Anna and Jordan.

TIMELINE OF JASVINDER'S LIFE

1951	Chanan Singh arrives in Derby, UK, from Kang Sabhu, Punjab.
1955	Chanan Singh returns to Punjab.
1957	Chanan Singh returns to Derby, bringing wife and family with him.
1965 (September)	Jasvinder born, Derby.
1981 (August)	Jasvinder runs away to Newcastle with Jassey Rattu. Disowned.
1984	Jasvinder marries Jassey. They settle in Bradford.
1985	Natasha born.
1987	Jasvinder and Jassey buy a house in Pudsey, away from Asian area.
1989	Jasvinder's sister Robina commits suicide.
1990	Jasvinder returns to Derby and buys house with Jassey.
1991	Jasvinder leaves Jassey.

1992	Mother dies.
1993	Jasvinder marries Rajvinder Sanghera. Anna born. Jasvinder takes A levels.
1994	Karma Nirvana founded. Jasvinder starts degree at Derby University.
1996	Karma Nirvana gets funding from National Lottery.
1997	Jasvinder splits from Rajvinder. Jordan born. Jasvinder graduates from Derby University (First Class Honours), buys her own house in Oakwood (suburb of Derby).
1999	Father dies.
2000	Jasvinder moves back into Asian area of Derby.
2004	Jasvinder moves to village outside Derby.
2007	*Shame* published. Honour Network Helpline established.
2008	Jasvinder receives Woman of the Year award. The Forced Marriage Act passes into law.
2009	*Daughters of Shame* published. Jasvinder receives Pride of Britain Award and an Honorary Doctorate from University of Derby.
2010	Jasvinder and family leave Derbyshire. Later in the year, Jasvinder visits Kang Sabhu.

PROLOGUE

On Saturday mornings when I was a child, after a big family breakfast of curry and chapattis, Dad and I used to drive up to his allotment together. It was on Ascot Drive, at the edge of an industrial area of warehouses and small factories, well away from the busy Asian neighbourhood in the middle of Derby where we lived. As he drove along in the orange Ford Cortina with the black plastic seats and the windscreen wipers that didn't work, Dad would mutter to himself, nodding and shaking his head as if rationalising things.

He would mutter even more if Mum had been complaining about him not going to the *gurdwara*, the Sikh temple at the end of the road where she went every Saturday and most weekdays as well. 'Why do I need to go there to worship a God I don't believe in?' he would say. 'I leave that to you. Anyway, you only go there to gossip.' My mother hated it when he said that. She would storm out of the house slamming the door, leaving Dad standing there, his head wobbling.

All week Dad worked nights at the Qualcast foundry up the road, making parts for lawnmowers. So Saturday was his special time. His routine never changed. Every Friday evening he would be down in the Byron pub at the end of our street, drinking and playing cards with his mates, mainly Indian men who spoke Punjabi. Then, after a good night's sleep and breakfast he would head up to the allotment with me. My sisters could have come as well, if they had wanted to, but they weren't bothered. I loved it. When Dad said he was going I would always jump up.

There were two great big rusty iron gates at the entrance, which swung outwards. When we arrived it was my job to get out of the car and pull them open. Once inside, Dad would park the Cortina on the dirt circle and lock the gates again. Then we would walk over together to his patch. It wasn't a bad size, probably twenty feet by forty, with a shed at one end. On one side there were mounds of soil and then in the middle, all the vegetables Dad was growing. Potatoes, in neat rows. Onions. Radishes, which we would have in our chapattis. Tomatoes. Marrows. Once he grew a marrow so huge that it was the talk of the allotments. I remember him calling people over to look at it.

Dad and I would work together, doing whatever needed to be done. Digging, planting, hoeing, weeding, watering, staking up new plants. It was hard work, but Dad always seemed at his happiest doing it. He came alive up there, getting his hands dirty, working with the soil.

When we were finished for the day he would sit outside the shed in his battered old deckchair, smoking a cigarette, sipping at a glass of whisky, or *desi*, the fiery Indian spirit that he and his friends distilled themselves. As the light faded, I sat on the ground beside him, crumbling the loose earth through my fingers as I listened to his stories of the past, the air around us tangy with the smell of leeks and onions. He would tell me about the place he came from, the Punjab.

'The breadbasket of India, *putt*. It covers only one and a half per cent of the surface area of the country, yet it provides two thirds of India's grain. Remarkable, eh?'

Dad would always speak to me in Punjabi, the language we used at home. Even by the end of his life he had only picked up the smattering of English he needed to get by at the factory and on the streets. My mother didn't speak English at all.

Dad's village was called Kang Sabhu, and as a child I used to picture it as a bigger version of the allotment, a place where Dad had been happy. On his bit of land, he told me, there was a huge shady tree, where at the end of the day the men would sit and talk, chewing sugar cane and cooling themselves with big wooden fans.

'Would I have sat there with you, like I do here?' I would ask.

'Goodness me, no. In the daytime, when your chores were done, you might have played under the tree. But in the evening your place would be back home, with the women.' If Dad had stayed in India, he continued, and I had grown up there, I would have been helping my mother with the household chores, grinding the grain, or perhaps looking after my little sister Lucy, while Mum fetched water from the village well in the big bronze pot that was far too heavy for children to carry.

Water had been precious then, Dad explained. It wasn't something that gushed easily out of a tap. Before he left India for good, in the late 1950s, there was no such thing as an irrigation system for the crops. There was the village well and that was that. You walked in the heat across the fields to fetch what water you needed. Ploughing was done with bullocks – and some of them could be stubborn, obstinate creatures, not like the tractors they had over there these days. As for his cows, he would be up early every morning to milk them, before carrying his churns into the village to be sold. 'I was a milkman in India,' he used to joke to me.

It was because life had been so hard that Dad decided as a young man to leave India and bring his wife and young family to England, where the story was that the streets were paved with gold: there were jobs that paid good wages, there was free education for children, there was free healthcare – for Dad and his fellow migrants such benefits were very real. As members of the Commonwealth, they would be accorded full rights of residence in the UK. Dad hadn't imagined he would spend the rest of his life here. His plan was to make money and then return.

Dad wasn't the only Punjabi who took the initiative to come over to fill the unskilled jobs in industry that there weren't enough English people to do after the Second World War. He told me how he and the other hopefuls set off from their villages in their crisp white cotton shirts and *salwar kameez*, the loose, pyjama-like garments worn by Punjabis of both sexes. When they reached the coast, they boarded the boat to England. To keep themselves amused, he and the other men danced the *bhangra* on deck, the wild traditional dance that was normally part of the celebrations for harvest. Dad played the *dhol*, the Asian drum, beating out the rhythm. I loved to imagine Dad doing this, with earrings in his ears; it was an image far removed from the quiet and serious man in drab brown clothes I was used to at home.

Of course, when he got to Derby, Dad soon discovered that things were not in fact quite like that 'paved with gold' fairy tale. There were, as promised, jobs at the foundries, but finding a place to stay wasn't easy. What he and his friends had heard about the UK was one thing; on the ground they were not as welcome as they had expected. Landlords were unwilling to rent to people of colour. There were signs in the windows of guest houses that read NO IRISH, NO BLACKS. People stopped talking when they went into shops or pubs. Even though Dad came from India he was lumped together with all the other Asian immigrants as a 'Paki'. Once, he was even ordered off a bus.

For the first five years he was on his own over here. He had left my mother back in Kang Sabhu. She was his second wife, the younger sister of his first, who had died from a snakebite. As was the custom, Mum had no choice in the matter of her life partner. At the age of fifteen she was told that this was the man she was going to marry, her dead sister's husband. As well as Dad, she also took on the care of the child from that first marriage, a little girl called Bachanu (in Punjabi pronounced *Budge-en-or*).

When Mum finally came over to the UK, late in the 1950s, she brought the three children she'd had with my father: Prakash, Ginda and my brother Balbir. Bachanu was left behind; by that stage she was married, so there was no question of her coming too. Instead she stayed with her new husband, Gurdial, in India. In my mind, she was always an intriguing mystery. I had once seen a black and white photo of her, but what was she really like? 'You'll meet her one day,' my father told me. He meant, of course, when I got married and, like the rest of my sisters, was taken back to the Punjab by my mother for the traditional wedding celebrations.

But then, as I have described in my book *Shame*, I never did get married to the man my parents intended me for, the man who stood in the middle of the group of other strangers in the photograph on the mantelpiece, the man who was *shorter than me*, whose name I never knew. At the age of fifteen-and-three-quarters I ran away from home with Jassey, a Sikh of a different, lower caste from us *jatts* – a *chamar*. By doing that I disgraced myself in the eyes of my family and my community. I never saw Kang Sabhu and I never met Bachanu.

As for Dad, though he had always planned to go back to Kang Sabhu one day to live, things didn't work out that way. When he and my mother had finally married off all their other six daughters and their one son, they were faced with a new responsibility: Sunny, the young son of my older sister Robina, who tragically committed suicide by setting herself on fire. Sunny brought both my parents much happiness in their final years, but he also put paid to any idea they might have had of going back to India for good.

Dad was an old man before he returned to Kang Sabhu, even for a holiday. When he did, he took Sunny with him

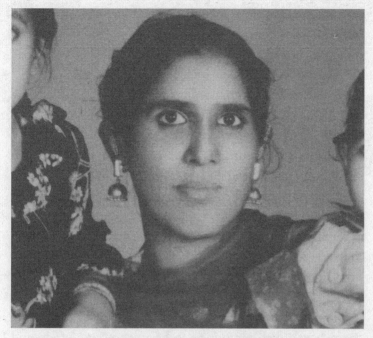

My mother in India, aged about twenty.

and the visit was a great success. Everyone in the village came out to meet them and they celebrated his return with a great feast. I would love to have been there with them, to have seen that oft-imagined landscape of my childhood in my father's company, to have stood together under that shady tree where he and his friends sat chatting in the evening. My mother had died by then, and I was back on some sort of speaking terms with him; but it still took me weeks to pluck up the courage to ask him whether I could go too. When I did his answer was all too clear. 'Shame travels, Jasvinder,' was the English version of his words. In Punjabi it came out longer. 'I can't do that,' he said. 'If you go with me, people will find out what you did. And when they do, your shame – your *bezti* – will taint them over there, too. I cannot be a party to that. You don't do our shame over in India like you have here in the UK.'

My father had no malice in his voice when he said these words, but for me it was as if a big door had finally been closed, right in front of me. Was I really so bad, twenty years after I'd been disowned, that I was still not worthy to sit among our Indian relatives and be accepted?

At another level, of course, I did understand. How could he explain who I was? Where was my husband? Why had I never been to India to get married like the others? Where did I sit in the order of things? I could imagine the questions flooding in and poor Dad struggling to answer them. But I still felt cheated.

I have no doubt my father loved me. But the only way he could have taken me out to India to show me off would have been if I was married to the man I'd been promised to. That doesn't bear thinking about. By now I would have had five of his children round my ankles and had to invite half his family over to the UK to live. I would probably be going out to India to arrange my own children's marriages, just as my mother did, the proud matriarch from England, with honour intact. I'm sure they would have been in demand, too, with their British passports the main draw.

After Dad came back from India I asked him about his trip; he told me how much he had enjoyed being there, how happy he was to have seen Bachanu again after so many years.

'Dad,' I asked, 'why didn't you go back to India before?'

'Because you were all born here. We had to stay.'

'Would you go back now?'

'I can't,' he replied, and there were tears in his eyes.

Later I asked him whether if he went again he would consider taking me, but his answer was the same. He could never go with me to India, he said. As it happened, that visit with Sunny was his last. He died in Dale Road, Derby, a couple of years later, far away from that shady tree and Kang Sabhu.

I

A strange thing happened to me as I checked into the flight at Heathrow this morning. I was showing my passport and boarding card to the security official, on my way to put my hand luggage through the scanner. She was Asian, good-looking, in her mid-thirties, I would guess. She looked at my passport and then back up at me. For a moment I thought there was a problem.

Then: 'Jasvinder Sanghera,' she said. 'You saved my life.'

I thought, *What*?

She said, 'I read your book *Shame* and because of your story I found the courage to leave my husband. He would have killed me if I hadn't gone.'

I was so taken aback, I didn't know what to say. There were people waiting in the queue behind me, but this passport officer didn't seem to mind about that. She said, 'I was born in England. I was forced to marry this man. My parents took me to Toronto for the wedding. He was awful, abusive and bullying. It was horrific.

There were so many times when I thought I was going to die.'

She reeled off this story to me and I just stood there. Then she said, 'I follow you in the news. You must keep doing what you're doing, because you save lives.'

'Thank you,' I said. I had no idea what else to say. She had the most beautiful broad smile and I couldn't imagine her ever being in a place where she feared death. I gave her my card and told her to get in touch. Even as I was aware that we were holding people up and I had to get on the plane, I wanted to see her again, to hear her story properly. Maybe she could testify for me, or get involved with Karma Nirvana, the charity I set up in 1994, which is dedicated to helping victims and survivors of forced marriage and honour-based violence.

I pressed her hand and went on through to Security. I felt recharged. I was thinking, This is what it's all about. This is why I go on doing what I do.

I do find it hard to switch off sometimes. Once through Security, walking around the duty free area on my way to the boarding gate, I noticed, as I always do in airports, lots of young Asian girls. It sounds ridiculous, but I always want to go up to them and ask them if they're OK. There they are with their parents or families and probably it's my imagination working overtime. They're most likely going off on a perfectly innocent holiday. But I still find myself looking hard at their faces and wondering if they're all right. Because if they are going to be taken back to India or Pakistan for a forced marriage, it's their families that will be taking them.

Obviously it's not my place to go up to them, but I did the next best thing, which was to put Karma Nirvana stickers on the backs of doors in every toilet that I could see at the airport. So what if I get caught, I thought. If we save just one more girl from a life of misery, that's enough for me.

Once we were actually up in the air it was really strange. I felt like I was reliving the experience of my sisters, making this same journey to India to be married all those years before. I felt as if I was in the seat with Ginda and Yasmin and Robina and Lucy. I started to feel frustrated on their behalf. I was thinking, Why didn't they go and tell somebody what was happening – one of the stewardesses or something? But no. They were just fifteen or sixteen, still children really. Mum was a powerful woman; she only had to give you one glance for you to know you couldn't say anything. My sisters would have been next to her on the plane, and she would have made very sure they were going to get there in one piece – a prize to be taken home and wed.

While Dad only dreamed of returning, Mum used to go to India every year; generally around October, which was the best time of year to travel to the Punjab, when the days were still pleasantly warm, but the nights were cooler. She would go on her own and return home laden with suitcases crammed with treasures. Dad would pick her up from the airport, and as she stepped out of the Ford Cortina and came through the front door of our little house in Normanton Road, she would bring the smell of India with her: a spicy mix of cumin and coriander, turmeric and cardamom, sandalwood, Neem hair oil and who knew what else. It hung heavily on the air of any room she stepped into. It was weeks before it was finally gone.

We four younger daughters – Yasmin, Robina, Lucy and I, the ones who had been born in the UK – would sit in a row on the sofa bed in the front room, eyes wide as saucers as Mum squatted on her heels beside her great big cases and started bringing out what she'd brought back: yards and yards of silks, unravelling through her fingers in brilliant colours, purples and scarlets and greens and yellows like you'd never see at home. Then scarves and saris decorated with the most beautiful embroidery: birds, flowers, intricate leaf patterns. I longed to reach out and touch them, to feel the gorgeous fabrics between my fingers. But I knew Mum wouldn't like that, so I kept my hands where they were, trapped safe under my legs.

Then came items for the kitchen: special stainless-steel plates and cups that shone like silver, Indian cooking implements, and food that Mum couldn't get here in the UK: big tins of ghee and jars of mango pickle that would be stacked on a high shelf and eked out over months for special occasions. There were strange orange sticks that looked to me like strips of bark, which Mum and Dad used to clean their teeth. There was jewellery: heavy gilt neck-lances, bracelets glittering with semi-precious stones, rings, anklets. Mum pulled them all out and they sat there like a sparkling puddle in her lap. She tried one on, knocking her bun crooked in her eagerness.

'Just wait until your Auntie Zeeta sees me wearing this,'

My mother at home in Derby.

she said, holding out her arms so we could all admire a string of amethysts glinting over her tired old cardigan.

She would talk more on the evening of her arrival than she normally did in a week. The words just kept pouring out: where she'd bought this, the price she'd paid for that, the scandalous amount she'd been charged for a *lassi* – us kids just sank back and luxuriated in her happiness. Dad would be there too, of course, polishing his glasses, head nodding from side to side as he listened in silence.

When Mum had finished setting everything out, transforming the dull brown carpet in our front room into something from a distant and wondrous world, Dad said, 'Better than the bazaar, eh, girls?' and we all smiled back at him, even though we had no idea what the bazaar looked like. All we knew was the Co-op at the end of our street.

Finally there would be plastic bottles of holy water from the Golden Temple at Amritsar, the most sacred shrine in the Sikh world. Mum showed us postcards of it and it looked amazing: the central temple, burnished with real gold, gleaming in the sunshine, reflected in the huge, blue-green pool that surrounded it. Guru Nanak, the founder of the Sikh religion, had meditated there, back in the fifteenth century, when it was still just a natural lake, and later gurus had built the temple on the site. In our house there were pictures of Guru Nanak everywhere. I grew up looking at his long white beard, thick eyebrows and heavy-lidded eyes under his yellow turban. Early every morning, Mum would switch on her prayers – *ik-oan-kaar, ik-oan-kaar, ik-oan-kaar* – and while this chant proclaiming that 'God is one' wailed round the house, waking us all up, she lit an incense stick in front of Guru Nanak's image. As the smoke swirled towards the ceiling she would pray. Then she would get back on her feet, open her bottle of holy water and sprinkle it round the room – and on us children too, if we appeared.

Weeks after Mum's return, bulky misshapen parcels of brown paper tied up with string would arrive. Unwrapped, they contained embroidered Punjabi quilts – *rajai* – which carried that same exotic Indian smell. In winter they were put on our beds and they were so heavy you felt as if you were pinned to the mattress. Robina and I would shove our heads under them and breathe deeply of that heady mix of spices, imagining we were far, far away from drab old Derby.

It feels strange, standing in a line that says FOREIGN PASSPORTS. My father was born in this country. Shouldn't the authorities somehow recognise that? Then I think how this wait must have been even stranger for Dad, who also had to stand in this queue when he came over here at the end of his life. Forced to choose between an Indian and a British passport he chose a British one. He ended up as a foreigner in his native land.

Even from this side of the barrier, already I can smell that familiar Indian smell. It brings the memory of my mother straight back to me in a rush. There's a smoky element to it, too. Through the windows of the aeroplane as we landed on the dark runway I could see the airport lights haloed in a pale misty smog. That was the first thing to hit my lungs as I stepped out into the warm Delhi night.

I'm excited and – yes, I must admit it – terribly apprehensive. I have thought about this trip for so long and now I'm actually doing it. I am going back to Kang Sabhu. On my own. To see for myself the landscape my father talked about, to see if I can find my sister Bachanu.

Apart from my children, nobody in my family knows I'm making this journey. I suspect that if my sister knew they would try and stop me. Maybe they would call Bachanu and tell her not to receive me. Maybe worse. Believe me, anything is possible So my visit has to be a total surprise.

If I do manage to find Bachanu, my greatest fear is that she won't see me. My father was clear enough. 'Shame travels,' he said. He knew the attitudes of the rural people here. I certainly don't want to bring trouble to my Indian family and I am hoping that things will be different now. But how much change is it realistic to expect, in just ten years? Maybe I am setting myself up for a huge humiliation – or worse.

But I need to do this. I long to see Kang Sabhu and I am desperate to make a connection with the one member of my family who has not rejected me. This is not just for me, but for my children. The sad fact is that they have been disowned just as much as I have. As the result of a decision their mother made when she was fifteen years old, they've got a big blank in their lives where an extended family should be. I don't regret that decision, it has enabled them to lead the lives they have today, but it's a pity that they never knew their grandparents, that even today they have living, breathing aunties and uncles and cousins who don't and won't speak to them.

I would also like my children to know and understand about my heritage, which is their heritage. Natasha, Anna and Jordan are second-generation British-born, but I still want them to be able to take their Asian past on with them into their British future. Not that I need worry about my eldest daughter, Natasha; she's already well into it. She wears Asian clothes, eats Asian food, listens to Asian music.

Natasha is getting married next year. Her husband-to-be, Anup, is a lovely fellow from a huge UK Asian family. It's a love match and despite the fact that I've spent my life

Natasha and Anup.

telling her not to get involved with Asian men, I couldn't be happier about it. But she wants a traditional Asian wedding, so all his relatives will be there. At the moment, in the absence of my family, our side will be represented by me and my children. That's fine. But wouldn't it be wonderful if I could get Bachanu over to the UK for the wedding too. Maybe it's a mad dream, but I would love to see her take on a proper role on Natasha's big day, bringing to life all the rituals I don't fully understand, that my mother would have explained and passed on to me at my own wedding if I hadn't run away and been disowned.

It was always Mum who took my sisters out to India to get married. On this journey the big suitcases would be laden with things from the prosperous UK: blankets, watches, and of course medicines: antibiotics and Paracetamol and all sorts. There was no NHS over there. Then there would be clothes for Bachanu and her children. All our cast-offs, no matter how tatty. Sometimes I would have something with holes in it and want to throw it away, but Mum always insisted Bachanu would find a use for it. 'She needs these things,' she'd say. 'She's very poor. We have to help her.'

I was too young to be aware of my oldest sister Prakash's wedding. So Ginda, the next one down, who brought us young ones up and was like a second mother to me, was the first sister I clearly remember getting married. She and Mum vanished for three months. I cried when she went and I was so excited when I knew she was coming back. But on her return she had completely changed. She had a wedding ring on and she was dressed differently, in a more grown-up way, in smart *salwar kameez,* with flashy jewellery. She used to go out to the shops in bare feet. I would ask her why she wasn't wearing shoes and she would say, 'This is what they do in India.'

At the same time she seemed more subdued. There was no more fooling around with us younger ones in front of the TV. Instead she and my mother would be talking in serious voices about this new husband – Shinda – who was coming over soon; meanwhile Ginda worked hard at the Reckitt and Colman shampoo factory up the road to save money and also so she could sponsor Shinda's visa. Then the local community leader arrived at the house with application forms to be filled in. To satisfy the immigration authorities, Mum and Dad had to prove it was a genuine marriage, that my sister and Shinda had lived together in India before she returned. That was why they had been gone so long.

After a year or so, Shinda arrived in Derby. Ginda left home and went to live a few streets away with her husband, his brother and his wife, who were already here. I missed her dreadfully. I used to ask Mum if we could go and visit her, but Mum was adamant. 'You don't go and visit your sister in her new husband's house,' she would shout at me. 'That is her home now.' That was the way it was. Ginda had started a new life. Once she had been the sister who'd plaited our hair and cooked dinner and protected us from Mum when she was hitting us – now she was someone I only saw at weddings.

As each of my sisters came up to the age of sixteen, I watched this same process repeated: a photo appeared, a trunk got filled, and away they went to India for a while.

The next one to go was Yasmin. As a girl she had been less respectful of the rules than Ginda. Mum had always taught us that we weren't allowed to make eye contact with men; and when men, even from our extended family, came to our house we had to sit in a separate room from them. But Yasmin pushed the boundaries. As a teenager she used to stand by our front door and flirt with the pop man, the young Asian guy who delivered bottles of Alpine Lemonade to our house on Sunday. Other times she would get dressed up in Western clothes and sneak out, covering short skirts and low tops with her school coat. 'Don't you dare say anything to Mum and Dad,' she'd say to us younger ones, who watched with awe.

But when it came to her marriage, Yasmin too went through with it without question. Her husband to be, Avtar, was the younger brother of Prakash's husband, Bila. The older generation liked it like that, keeping things in families. So once again, shortly after Yasmin's sixteenth birthday, there was the photograph, the big trunk, and then the trip with Mum to India. When she returned she still made eyes at the pop man while the immigration forms were being filled in, but it wasn't long before Avtar arrived and off she went with him to her new life in London, staying at first with Prakash and his brother.

The next sister to be married was Robina, just two years older than me. She didn't go through with it so easily. Shortly before she was supposed to leave for India, she ran away one evening and none of us could find her. Eventually it was me that discovered her, hiding in the outside toilet at the bottom of the garden. She was huddled on the seat crying her eyes out.

'I can't do it,' she was saying. 'I'm too young. I don't want to get married to this man.'

'Let's run away together,' I said, as I clasped her hand tight. I meant it too, even though I was just thirteen at the time.

'Don't be silly,' she replied. 'I couldn't do that. That would be it. Mum would never accept me back in the family . . .'

Eventually she came into the house. As I went upstairs I could hear my mother shouting at her; I think she and my father really thought Robina had run away. From our bedroom I could hear her sobbing and pleading with them. 'Please,' she was crying, 'I don't want to marry this man I don't know . . .' After that, until she finally went, I begged her not to do it. 'You don't have to go through with it,' I told her. 'You could still run away.' But my mother was more cunning than I was. Robina was told that she could go to India and see what she thought of the country and her husband-to-be when she got there. If she didn't like it, or him, then she could always change her mind. But of course it didn't work out like that, did it? Robina was married off just like all the others.

She was gone so long that when she returned they had to put her into my year in school because she'd missed so much work. Even though she was now in my class, again there was the same transformation. Before she had gone, Robina and I had been best friends. We'd watch *Charlie's Angels* and do pretend karate running around the house. On her return all that stopped. As a married woman, she couldn't be seen doing such things, she told me. She went to school wearing *salwar kameez*, not her school uniform any more. The next thing I knew she was off to join her husband Navtej in Germany. Mum and Dad hadn't managed to get a visa for him to come to England, so she had to go there. As she packed to leave, she was sobbing. Me too. We were like a parting couple. When she got to Germany I sent her a Michael Jackson CD, which included the song 'One Day In Your Life', much played on the radio around that time. It was my attempt to try and explain how I was feeling.

Just call my name
And I'll be there

From my perspective as a girl growing up, seeing each of my sisters get married was like watching lambs go to the slaughter. But I would never have continued to think that if these marriages between my sisters and the men chosen for them had been happy – or had even worked out at any level. But they weren't – and they didn't. As a young, impressionable girl I heard, over and over again, the tearful phone calls Mum got from the newlyweds and her stoical replies. 'That's what marriage is like . . .' 'It's your duty . . .' 'Don't you *dare* to disgrace us.' Bundled into the car and taken over to see the new husband in the new house, I would sit cross-legged on the floor witnessing the tense sessions between Mum and whichever sister it was we were visiting. Once us women were alone, the complaints would flow. Her husband had shouted at her because his dinner wasn't hot. He wouldn't let her go to the baby when it was crying at a meal. 'Every day there's something. Why should I put up with it?'

'Because he's your husband,' Mum would reply.

'He drinks too much. Then he gets aggressive with me.'

'A man likes his drink. You must learn to be a little calmer.'

Mum always took the husband's side. 'A man is like a hot pan of milk,' she said. 'You have to be careful it doesn't boil over. When it gets to the top your job as a woman is to blow on it and cool it down.'

When I was fourteen and I had the audacity to spend some money I'd saved from a paper round getting my hair cut and permed in a Western style, I was punished by being sent away to stay with my oldest sister Prakash in London for a while. The idea was that I would learn some respect and how to be a more dutiful daughter. But what actually happened was that I witnessed Prakash's marriage at first hand. Her husband Bila was a strong young man who looked a bit like Elvis Presley. He had livid yellow eyes, like the devil's, I always thought, though in fact they were a symptom of the liver poisoning that eventually killed him. When he was out of the house at his job at the Mother's Pride factory, everything was OK. But then he would return and start drinking his whisky and he would get more and more aggressive. Prakash was very strict with us children and would discipline her three sons – Manjit, Ranjit and Baljit – with a stick. But she was no match for Bila. The more he drank the more he shouted at her. Then he would shove her around and slap her too sometimes. Even though I was scared of Prakash, I felt sorry for her. Once, Bila beat her up so badly that she came back home to Derby and had to go to hospital. Despite all that, Mum still talked her into returning to her husband, and back she dutifully went.

Ginda's problems weren't as bad as Prakash's; but on the few occasions she came over from her house in Depot Street to visit us it was clear she wasn't happy either. Shinda didn't drink as much as Bila, but I think he too used to beat her. She had bruises that she would show to Mum; and of

Me in my school uniform with my late sister, Robina.

course Mum would try and talk her round, tell her that this was what marriage involved.

Once again, I saw all this at first hand, because when I came back from staying with Prakash in London, I lived with Ginda for a while. I think Mum thought that my older sister might be able to teach me to be a better Asian girl, but instead all I saw was another clear view of the kind of marriage I didn't want for myself. When she wasn't at work at the shampoo factory, Ginda cooked and cleaned for Shinda. On Friday and Saturday nights, or Sunday afternoons, he would come home drunk with all his friends, expecting a meal. I used to help her, racing around cooking curry and chapattis for all these noisy men. Shinda thoroughly approved of me in this role. He often said to me,

'You cook really well. I have a nephew that you're going to marry one day.' He also liked that I was good with his little boy, David. That was another sign of the kind of dutiful wife that was required.

It was a similar story with Avtar, Yasmin's husband. Like his elder brother Bila, he drank too much and Yasmin wasn't happy with him. But she didn't put up with the marriage forever. She subsequently divorced Avtar and married another man. She took her two sons with her and had two more girls. Avtar was gutted when she left him. His drinking got worse and he ended up killing himself.

Because Robina went to live in Germany with her husband Navtej, I didn't get to witness her marriage first hand. But from the phone conversations she had with Mum, I knew that she too was unhappy. You could hear her complaining and crying, then Mum would say, 'No, Robina, you have to stay there now. That's your home.'

I used to beg my mother to let me speak to her, and Mum would always say, 'You can talk to her, but don't ask her anything.' She meant about the marriage, or how she was in herself. And Mum would stay right by the phone, to make sure I didn't put the wrong questions or get too personal. The message was clear: Robina's marriage was her own affair, not to be shared with us.

Then Robina and Navtej moved to Canada to be near Navtej's brother. Things didn't improve. Robina kept on ringing Mum and telling her Navtej was beating her up. Mum's answer was always the same. 'I will talk to your husband.' But that didn't work either, because when she did finally say something, Navtej gave her a serious piece of his mind. His attitude was, how dare you speak to me about how to keep my wife and run my affairs. Mum never tried that line again. In the end Robina ran away. She took their son, Sunny, who was just a tiny baby, jumped on a plane, and came back to Derby to live with Mum and Dad. They didn't try and send her back after that. They took her in.

By that stage I had run away myself, so maybe their acceptance of Robina had something to do with a change in their attitudes as a result of that. Or maybe, after Mum had been spoken to by Navtej in that way she was readier to take Robina's side. At any rate, Robina and Sunny lived with my parents for a while, until her divorce came through, at the family house in Dale Road.

I would seriously love to be able to say that one of my sisters' arranged marriages was happy, but that wasn't the case. Even Lucy, my younger sister, who married the man I was intended for, Shinda's nephew, didn't have any joy. I felt for her in particular, because after what I'd done, I thought maybe I might have paved the way for her to object. Certainly she was given much more freedom by my parents before she married than I'd ever had. I remember the first time after I'd run away that I met up with her, in secret, in Markeaton Park, a big open space in Derby that is well away from the Asian area. Her hair was cut in a short, sleek bob. She was wearing a fashionable Western skirt and fitted blouse. I was shocked – I would never have been allowed to dress like that. This look was the symptom of a far laxer parental regime. Lucy was allowed out with her friends, to the pub, even clubbing, she told me. At the time I remember feeling gutted – her freedom seemed to me to make a mockery of everything I'd been through. But that jealousy didn't last when she went ahead with her marriage.

The family couldn't organise a visa for her husband to come to the UK, so like Robina she went to join him in Germany. I was living in my own place by then, so there were no restrictions on what I could ask Lucy or what she could tell me over the phone. It soon all came tumbling out: she wasn't happy, she didn't want to be with this man, she couldn't cope. She told me she was going to ring Mum to complain and I thought, 'Here we go again.' Sure enough, when Lucy called back it was, 'Mum doesn't listen. She just tells me I've got to make it work.'

'Of course she does,' I told her. 'That's always been her attitude.'

Even though I had only just started speaking to my mother again, after five long years of non-communication, I thought I had to take a risk for Lucy. 'Look, I'll ring her,' I said and I did. But Mum was unwavering. 'If you ever want to talk to me again,' she said, 'you will tell Lucy to stay there and make it work with her husband.'

'I can't do that, Mum,' I said. 'I can't tell her to stay there with a man who is treating her so badly.'

'Well then, I will never talk to you again,' Mum replied.

I told Lucy what Mum had said. She wasn't going to get any help from that direction.

Then I would get calls that really scared me. Lucy would phone me, then suddenly cut off mid-conversation, as if someone had just walked into the room. I had no idea what was going on, but whatever it was it wasn't good. Finally she turned up on my doorstep in Bradford out of the blue, carrying nothing more than a suitcase. She had saved up her airfare in secret and, like Robina, just run away. Thank God there were no children involved.

The only one of us who was allowed to be with the partner he wanted was my brother Balbir. He had been with Dawn since he was a teenager, when my mother used to go round to her house and bang on her door to get Balbir to come home. Dawn's dad was Asian, but her mother was white, and Mum used to call her a 'half-caste', among other insults. My parents always made it clear they didn't approve of the relationship, but in the end they allowed them to be married. Balbir was a boy, after all, and boys were always treated differently in our community.

2

Now I am settled into a nice quiet guest house in South Delhi. After just a couple of hours' sleep, I was woken by the distinctive wail of the Muslim call to prayer. This was the dawn call, the first of five during the course of the day. I fell back to sleep and woke in time for a late breakfast – and what a breakfast it is! The smell takes me straight back to my childhood in Derby.

On the table is a big pile of *mooli paratha*, the chapattis filled with those same tangy radishes my father used to grow on the allotment. There are pickles and fresh yoghurt to go with it, as well as several spicy vegetarian curry dishes, like *saag aloo* and potatoes with chillis. All washed down with little glass cups of *chai*, the sweet milky Indian tea flavoured with cardamom. Mum used to put the *chai* on at six in the morning and you could smell it across the house as it bubbled away. At weekends she would make the *mooli paratha* too, and we kids would sit around the table eating them, all of us sisters chattering and laughing.

I text my daughter Natasha in the UK to tell her I've arrived and am settling in fine. She badly wanted to come with me on this trip, but I had to say no to her. She is twenty-five now, and perfectly able to look after herself. But as a parent my job is to protect her and, whatever she thinks, I would still have been worried about her personal safety. The fact is, I have no idea what I'm going to be getting into up in rural Punjab. I have no idea what the place will even look like. My father spoke of a land of open fields and bullock carts, of men who sat chatting all evening under a spreading, shady tree. I am hardly expecting it to be like that now, half a century later. But how will it be?

I am here without Natasha, but I'm not alone. Two men I trust have agreed to accompany me on my quest. The first travelled out to Delhi with me. Tony Hutchinson was a senior policeman with the Cleveland CID when I first met him four years ago. He stood out from many other policemen I've met and worked with over the years by taking a serious and active interest in forced marriage. He was alerted to the issue by reading a piece about my book *Shame* in a Sunday newspaper. He decided to attend a Karma Nirvana conference. Later, he told me that when he got home that evening he couldn't sleep. In his 28 years in the police force he had never come across forced marriage or honour killings, at least not described in those terms. But as he thought back through the many cases he had dealt with as a Detective Superintendent in the homicide squad, he started to wonder if he and his fellow officers had been missing something. He recalled one case of a young Asian woman who had doused her clothes in paraffin and set fire to herself in her kitchen, exactly as my sister Robina was supposed to have done; then the 'suicide' of another Asian woman who had gassed herself and her children in her car with carbon monoxide exhaust fumes. Was it possible these had been honour killings? Subsequently Tony contacted me, organised a police conference on forced marriage, and ended up setting up Choice Line, a police helpline for young Asian woman in his area. As well as a colleague in arms, Tony has since become a good friend. Tall, burly, and with thirty years of hands-on police experience, I am happy to have him along for the ride.

When we get up to the Punjab we are going to be joined by Natasha's fiancé Anup, known to his family and friends as Sunny. To avoid confusion with my nephew Sunny, I'll call him by his proper name of Anup (pronounced *Anoop*), though face to face he's always Sunny to me. The paradox is that if I had been looking for an arranged partner for Natasha, I could hardly have done better than Anup, who is also from a Punjabi Sikh background, and a caste (not that either of them care a hoot about such things) half-way between *chamar* and *jatt*. And how did they get together? Was it through some complex, old-fashioned negotiation of parents and aunties, working out exactly how appropriate they were for each other? No, they met at the Homebase superstore in Leeds, doing part-time jobs when they were students.

As luck would have it, Anup has an uncle in Jalandhar, which is the nearest big town to Kang Sabhu, so we will have some measure of family support up there and, if things go seriously wrong, somewhere to run to. Anup has been back and forth to the Punjab for years, he speaks better Punjabi than me, he is a man, and he's my future son-in-law. Surely my sister will be unable to resist my daughter's fiancé? It's great that he's made the effort to fly out here to be with me; I feel that whatever happens, he can only be an asset.

Before we set out on the big road trip north, I have some calls to make here in Delhi. It would have been a terrible missed opportunity for me to come all the way to India and not see what is happening on the ground here in regard to forced marriages. At home I have dedicated most of my working life to setting up and running Karma Nirvana, a charity which was founded with the stated aim of helping 'women with cultural and language barriers' and soon developed, as I'd intended, into providing support for victims and survivors of honour-based violence and forced marriage.

We aim to get involved at every stage, from the very first signs that honour-based abuse might be taking place within a family (a girl not being allowed to wear Western clothes or have friends from outside the Asian community, being refused a mobile phone, not being allowed a boyfriend and so on) through to helping girls who find themselves, as I did, at the age of fifteen-and-three-quarters, suddenly confronted with the reality that they are about to be forced into a marriage they don't want. Sometimes this may be within the UK, but all too frequently such marriages involve a trip to India, Pakistan or Bangladesh, where the victim suddenly discovers that the 'holiday' she thought she was going on is in fact her own wedding. As a young teenager, born and educated in the UK, she is being forced into a union with a man she has never met, who speaks a different language, and is from a completely different culture. Based on promises from birth, these matches are often also to much older men.

At Karma Nirvana we work hard to try and stop these dreadful marriages. We run the Honour Network Helpline, a nationwide service that victims and potential victims can phone in confidence, in the knowledge that they will be speaking to people entirely on their side, often survivors of forced marriages or attempts at forced marriage. If a situation is serious, we will intervene, alerting police or getting vulnerable young women (and young men, too, because around 15 per cent of our calls are from males) away from their families into refuges where they can start to rebuild their lives. But sometimes we are unable to do this. The victim has never heard of our helpline, is perhaps extremely isolated, doesn't have the confidence or courage to resist the will of their family and make that call, or is just taken by surprise and suddenly finds themselves on a plane, then on the ground out here, being driven by a parent or relative to some alien rural village from which there is no obvious means of escape.

So first stop for me today is the British High Commission, which since 2005 has run a Forced Marriage Unit that provides guidance and support for young people who find themselves in this dreadful trap. Both I and Karma Nirvana were active in campaigning for the Forced Marriage Unit and the legal teeth of that initiative, the Forced Marriage Act, so I feel more than a little involvement in this work.

The Act finally came into force in November 2008; it establishes for the first time in British law that a person threatened with a forced marriage can apply in court for an order to prevent such a union taking place. Forced marriage is still only a civil, not a criminal offence, but the Act is considerably better than nothing.

Even getting to this point was a long haul. When I ran away from home in 1981, there was little or no understanding of forced marriage among police or social services in the UK. It wasn't even recognised as a problem. Asian communities did things their way, as they had done for centuries, and that wasn't the business of UK agencies or lawmakers. Indeed, because there was always great sensitivity around the whole issue of immigration and how and whether immigrants were being assimilated, should be assimilated, or whether their culture had equal validity with any pre-existing 'British' one, etc, etc, this was one of many issues around Asian communities that had a large 'hands-off' notice attached to it.

For my own part, I was lucky enough to be saved by a kind Geordie policeman. Ten days after Jassey and I had fled from Derby in his purple Ford Escort, the police caught up with us in Newcastle, a city we had picked at random, but suitably far from home to offer us, we thought, a safe hiding place. How naive we were! It never occurred to us that the police might be able to find us through Jassey's car number plate. Early one morning there was a knock at the door and a tall, heavily-built, grey-haired copper stood before us. 'Jassey Rattu,' he said, 'I have reason to believe that you have abducted and are now harbouring a young lady, Jasvinder Kaur Kang. She went missing from her home in Derby ten days ago and has not contacted her family since. Her parents are very concerned for her safety.'

I broke down in tears and explained that abduction was very far from the case. Jassey had rescued me from a marriage that was my worst nightmare. My parents refused to listen to me, just as they had never listened to my sisters, who were now in dreadful abusive marriages they had never asked for. All I wanted was to be allowed to continue my education and, in due course, if I wished, to marry a man of my own choice. Fortunately – and incredibly, I see now – that nameless officer believed me and took our side.

'I've seen this before,' he told us. 'I understand your position and why you did what you did – and I'm not going to tell your parents where you are. What I will do is tell them you've contacted the police and you are safe.'

I can only imagine the frustration of my parents when the police called them to say that they knew where we were, but that they had decided to leave us alone. 'Good luck to you both,' this remarkable officer said as he left.

Others weren't so lucky. Girls who ran away from home were tracked down and returned to the families who had reported them missing, often with the blessing or assistance of the police or other authorities. The Asian community played its part as well; to an outsider, our subculture may seem large and disparate enough, but believe me it has its own networks: minicab drivers and corner shop owners who keep a beady eye out for all kinds of things, runaways included. The private detectives and bounty hunters who were – and still are – employed to track these girls down often have more help than the average white citizen would realise.

It wasn't until the deaths of some of these girls started to hit the news that the wider community and our legislators began to sit up and take notice. In 1999, after the murder of Rukhsana Naz, a 19-year-old woman from Derby who was strangled by her brother while her mother held her down, the MP Anne Cryer instigated a debate on the issue of forced marriage in the House of Commons. As a result of this, a working group was established, and in 2000 produced the first public report on forced marriage, *A Choice By Right*. Shortly after this, three more young women made news as victims of 'honour killings': Nuziat Khan, strangled in 2001 after she asked her husband Iqbal for a divorce; Heshu Yones, stabbed repeatedly by her father in 2002 because she dressed in Western clothes and had started a relationship with a Christian boy; and Anita Gindha, strangled in 2003 when eight and a half months' pregnant for trying to leave an arranged marriage to marry the man she loved.

By 2004 the Government had set up a Forced Marriage Unit in the UK and in 2005 there was a second report on the issue, *Forced Marriage: A Wrong Not A Right*. This was followed in December of that year by a debate on honour killings in the House of Lords. Finally, the Forced Marriage (Civil Protection) Act was introduced as a private member's bill into the House of Lords by Lord Lester of Herne Hill on 16 November 2006. It was passed by the House of Lords on 13 June 2007 and the House of Commons a month later, finally coming into force in

November 2008. (It came too late to help Arash Ghorbani-Zarin, stabbed 46 times in 2004 by the brothers of the girl who was carrying his baby; Samaira Nazir, stabbed 18 times in 2006 by her brother and cousin, because she wanted to marry for love; and Banaz Mahmod, strangled at the behest of her father and uncle in 2006, after she left a violent husband to start a relationship with the man of her choice.)

Many campaigners helped to achieve this result, but I hope both I and Karma Nirvana played our part. Lord Lester was sent a copy of *Shame* before it came out, and as a result came to visit Karma Nirvana in Derby. The book was distributed widely in Parliament and I was invited to sit in on several of the meetings where the Act was drafted. Many of the politicians – Lords, Baronesses and so on – had never met a survivor of forced marriage before, and were probably as bemused by me as I was by them. Lord Lester even invited me to the Second Reading of the Act in the Lords. Though I had been to the House several times by then, I had never been inside the chamber before. I took a survivor with me, a young woman who had recently been rescued by the Forced Marriage Unit from a marriage to a much older relative in Pakistan. We were both awestruck looking down at the rows and rows of plush red leather benches and at the centre of it all, the Queen's magnificent throne. It seemed a long way from that dingy bedsit in Newcastle where, for me, this story had started. For my companion too, it was an inspiring day: proof that anything is possible in this country if you work hard enough at it.

* * *

Even though Tony has passed several advanced driving courses back in the UK, he doesn't feel up to dealing with the crazy Delhi traffic. The three-lane highway into town is crowded with vehicles of all kinds: trucks, buses, cars, motorcycles, mopeds, not to mention the little yellow and green three-wheel auto-rickshaws, also known as *tuk-tuks*. There is no lane discipline and no clear rule of the road, except perhaps that most of the army of mopeds crowd into the slow lane (the men, exclusively, wear helmets and drive, while the women ride pillion, bare-headed, in saris). The whole road is like a giant dodgem track, where everyone is trying to get ahead no matter what, cutting each other up, squeezing into every available space, all to the accompaniment of a continual blaring of horns. But our taxi driver seems remarkably calm as he weaves expertly through the mayhem. How he gets through a day, let alone a week, without an accident, is a mystery.

In contrast to all this madness, the British High Commission is a green oasis of quiet, like a big park behind its high walls. Around the clean white modern consular buildings are exotic trees, many flowering, which I couldn't begin to name – though I do recognise the pink and white flowers of frangipani, the tall white-trunked, grey-green eucalyptus and of course the ubiquitous palm.

We are met by David Grahame, Consular Regional Director for South Asia, a genial thirty-something in loose grey trousers and a blue and white striped open-necked shirt: clearly a diplomat, but not in any way old-school. With him is his Asian colleague Dinesh Kumar, Head of the Delhi Consular Assistance Team, an older man with a fine semicircular moustache.

We sit at a round cast-iron table on a neatly-mown lawn and are offered coffee from the Embassy's own Costa outlet. It's a little bit of England in India, though somewhat warmer than mid-November at home, as sunny and congenial as a day in July. Some of the bird cries are harsher than you'd hear in an English garden and above us several kites wheel slowly on the rising air currents. Another creature you wouldn't see at home is the monkey that's being led by his handler around the compound on a long lead. He has a thick coat of fluffy yellow-white fur, long agile arms and legs, a splendid tail, and bright eyes in a cheeky dark face. As he munches thoughtfully on a leaf, his expression is all but human. He has an essential role at the High Commission, David explains, chasing off all the other monkeys who would otherwise invade this prize patch of green space.

David's responsibilities are for British subjects who get into trouble of all kinds across the South Asian region: this includes everything from lost passports, drunkenness and traffic offences, right through to those who get arrested for a serious crime. Tellingly, 25 per cent of their workload now has to do with Forced Marriage.

As head of the Forced Marriage Unit (FMU) at the High Commission, Dinesh has direct responsibility for this work in Delhi and right across the north of India. He talks me through the statistics. They have had over four hundred calls in the past year from young women and men who have found themselves in trouble in the South Asian region.

They have been actively involved in 170 cases. Their response varies from offering support on the phone through to driving out to remote villages and rescuing girls who are being held against their will by their extended families. In this last resort, they enlist the help of the local authorities, the police, the judiciary, and so on, who are, Dinesh tells us, generally very helpful. Their biggest problem may well be locating the place where the girl is being held; there are no postcodes in this part of the world. 'Often you have no more than a landmark to go on, the house next to this or that tree or shop in a particular village.'

When Dinesh and his team do turn up to these often very fraught situations, they never say that they are coming to rescue a girl from a forced marriage. Even though they always travel with armed police, that would be too dangerous. Instead, to get the victim away from the family, they have to exercise tact. The official story is generally that there is something wrong with the girl's passport, which is why she needs to return to the High Commission. Often, they are followed back to Delhi by a carload or two of relatives, who have to be got rid of once the victim is safely away from the threatening environment.

The girl at the centre of these situations will usually be petrified. She is unlikely to tell the truth about her situation to start with. Only when she is away from the family, safely in a room at the Embassy, is she likely to start giving Dinesh the real story of what's going on.

In my book *Daughters of Shame*, I tell the story of Mariam, rescued from under the noses of her gun-toting Pakistani family and whisked back to Islamabad pursued by carloads of relatives. She had been so badly whipped by her relatives that she couldn't sit up straight in the car. Such a case, Dinesh assures me, is still typical. Month in, month out, he is bringing girls back to safety from the hands of their families in far-flung villages in the north of India, just as his colleague Albert is in Pakistan. 'Jasvinder,' he says, 'I see these girls and I cannot understand why and how it continues to happen – they were born in England.'

It is fascinating for me to get this Indian perspective on the story. The work I do with Karma Nirvana in the UK stops at the airport. I can do my best to get girls out of situations where their families are trying to force them into a marriage they don't want. I can encourage them to make a stand and help them find police protection, refuge accommodation and, in cases of extreme danger, a new identity. But once that family has got them on the plane it's impossible to follow. That's why I find myself looking at Asian girls at airports. It's a feeling of powerlessness about these ongoing injustices.

But Dinesh and the Forced Marriage Unit have a real chance to make things happen over here in India, and it's a chance that they're acting on. Personally, I think that this statistic of four hundred people per year in the region is too low. My gut feeling is that there are many more out there, trapped in situations beyond their control, who don't perhaps realise that something as grand-sounding as the British High Commission is in a position to help them; that they can make a call and get a sympathetic, supportive response; that these kinds of hands-on rescues are not only possible, but happening right now.

When I tell Dinesh and David this, I'm encouraged by their response. Rather than poo-pooing my instincts and assuring me that they've got the whole situation under control, David agrees that there is a continuing problem with reaching the victims. 'The key thing for us,' he says, 'is raising awareness. We help, we rescue people, but we're always concerned for the cases we don't hear about. They need to know we're here.'

With this aim in mind, the Forced Marriage Units in both London and Delhi have run campaigns to try and alert potential victims to what they're doing in the UK and Asia; they distribute the *Survivor's Handbook*, a smartly-designed pamphlet with chapters on everything from the practicalities of ending a marriage, to where to live away from family, how to repay debts or find a job. They work very hard to let the victims who are undoubtedly out there know that there is help available. But of course, as David admits, they've only been working in this area for a few years and it is inevitably an ongoing process. 'I think we've come a long way,' he says, 'but I don't think anyone claims it's perfection yet.'

I'm impressed by what the High Commission is doing out in India, but I have a serious issue with the fact that once the girls have been returned to the UK, the provision for them is not what it should be. Rescued in alarming circumstances then sent home alone on a plane, when they get to Heathrow they are often not effectively supported. The relevant local authority or social services fail them and they can, I know for a fact, even find themselves back with the very families they've escaped from.

'So you've gone through all of that work to rescue them,' I say, 'and the victim has gone through all that trauma, only to be put back in the very situation they were running away from.'

One shocking example of the lack of joined-up thinking in this area is that the young people who are rescued by the High Commission are expected to pay for their airfare home. For a terrified fifteen or sixteen-year-old, traumatised by being suddenly separated from the family they've grown up with (and still love and depend upon emotionally), having to find the cash for their transport home is an extra burden they don't need; it may even, in my view, tip the balance from getting away from their abusers to not.

Both David and Dinesh acknowledge this issue as a problem. 'Once the victims leave us,' Dinesh admits, 'we have no idea what happens to them.' And yes, they have, they confirm, seen some girls come round more than once. They've said goodbye to them at the airport only to find, a few months later, that they've been brought back out here by their families. In some cases more than once. One girl they were aware of ran away three times. 'There's more we can do,' David acknowledges. 'We absolutely don't want people caught up in these cycles.'

I feel it's important that David and Dinesh understand that I'm speaking from experience here, so I decide that now is the time to tell them my own story. Even though I know that Dinesh runs this Forced Marriage Unit (so is surely on my side) it feels very strange for me to be sharing my experience with an Asian male. Back home, so many Asian men condemn what I did in running away and what

I do now with Karma Nirvana. Even when they claim to be broadly sympathetic to the cause, they are rarely support-ive in any practical way.

It's sad to say, but they are more likely to be like the Asian MEP I met when I was out at the European Parliament in Brussels last week. He was on the panel of a discussion I was taking part in about whether Muslims in Europe got overlooked as good citizens. At one point I put my hand up and raised the issue of young girls going missing from schools in the UK each summer to be taken out to Asia for forced marriages. It was a question clearly directed at him, but he refused to answer. His reaction was quite deliberate. As my colleague John from the EU said to me afterwards, you could almost see him squirm.

When the session was over, John and I were walking down a corridor when this same man appeared out of nowhere and made a beeline for me. 'Jasvinder! Jasvinder!' he was shouting, as if he'd known me for a long time. When I stopped he shook my hand and said, 'I just wanted to say that the work you are doing is absolutely brilliant. It really is a credit to you. Well done.' I was standing there think-ing, 'Why on earth couldn't you have said that in there? Why couldn't you at least have answered my question about the missing girls?'

'It's great you feel like that,' I replied. 'Maybe I could contact you and see how you can work with us on these important issues. Perhaps you can do something for us in the future in your role as an MEP.'

All of a sudden he went very cagey. 'Yes, yes,' he said, 'do write to me.'

'I will,' I said, 'because Karma Nirvana are going to be hosting events at the European Parliament on these issues very soon.' His face fell.

As he walked off, John laughed. 'You've scared him,' he said. 'Did you see the fear in his face when you said that?'

But Dinesh is not at all in this all-too-typical equivocal mode. As I talk them through my story, he is highly supportive and understanding, not to say shocked; not so much that I am a disowned woman, more that this all happened to me 28 years ago, long before the days of the Forced Marriage Unit and the High Commission being involved in rescues. Once again he makes the point: why does this happen in the UK? Why did emigrant families never adapt to the host culture?

When we break for lunch, Dinesh asks me whether I would like to go out into Delhi and see one of the refuges that the Forced Marriage Unit uses to house girls when they've been rescued, before they are returned back to the UK. I have no hesitation in saying yes.

Before we leave the High Commission, while Dinesh is sorting out transport for us, I go for a short stroll with David round the grounds.

'It's really enlightening for me,' I say, 'to come across people who are so willing to listen, who are not brushing difficult issues under the carpet. So many civil servants I deal with are black and white – it's almost like they've been trained never to say what they think. They're like robots who aren't in touch with the real world.'

David laughs.

'It makes my job easier to meet someone like you,' I tell

him. 'It feels like there's something that puts you in touch with this issue beyond what you've read and know from your work.'

He smiles. 'Jasvinder,' he says, 'I'm married to an Asian woman.'

'That's what it is. I knew there was something. Are you happily married?'

He looks a little taken aback.

'No, I don't mean happily married as in, "Are you happy together?" I mean, have her family accepted you?' It was the first thing that came into my head: white guy, Asian woman, where are the family?

'Her family are wonderful,' he says. 'I feel totally accepted.'

That is good to hear, and another useful counterbalance to the stories I'm so often faced with in my work. In my own life I'm lucky to have the example of Natasha and Anup, whose family have accepted and welcomed her as his partner, despite the fact that she's from a different caste and her mother is disowned. Even though they're not yet married, Natasha lives with Anup's family in their house. Coming from the background I did, I find that remarkable. It's also bizarre for me, because when Natasha was growing up, I always said to her, 'Whatever you do, don't go out with an Asian guy.'

Natasha used to laugh my interference off. 'Mum,' she would say, 'you can't say that, that's racist.'

But I was serious. In Asian communities, you don't just get involved with the man, you get involved with the family. 'What Asian family is going to accept you, Natasha?' I told her. 'You're mixed caste, you have a mother who was a runaway. You are always going to have a hard time for that. Save yourself all the hassle. Go out with a white man.'

But children always do the opposite of what you tell them. When she met Anup, as a student, Natasha fell for him despite my warnings. I'm glad she did. Their happiness has made me rethink the prejudices my experience has saddled me with.

I tell David this story about my daughter and he laughs. It's all too easy, he agrees, to let the shocking cases that we deal with professionally colour our view of the bigger picture.

'And now she wants a full-blown Asian wedding!' I say.

3

Dinesh takes us across town to a house in the suburbs that serves as the office of a non-governmental organisation called Swanchetan (which means 'Hope After Trauma' in Hindi). The organisation works to support survivors of trauma: from child abuse, sexual assault or relationship violence right through to kidnapping, human trafficking and terrorist attack. Part of their work involves British victims of forced marriage, who are counselled and offered refuge until they are ready to return to the UK.

Outside the bars of the front gate there's an armed policeman. Inside, a staircase leads to a first-floor landing with a view over a courtyard. Its salmon-pink walls are badly in need of a lick of paint. A bicycle wheel lies on a flat corrugated-iron roof; below, in the inner well of the house, the thick foliage of a climbing plant twines around a row of plastic water tanks.

We press an entryphone buzzer to the left of a thick steel door and are let into an office with blinds half-closed against the bright sunshine outside. Three or four women in saris sit at wooden desks talking on phones or working at bright computer screens. One of them greets Dinesh warmly and leads us through to a side room, where there's a long table surrounded by wooden chairs. On the wall behind is a picture of an elephant made from cut up post-cards. I notice framed positive affirmations everywhere. *Where there is shade there is sunshine* is one that brings a smile to my face. At Karma Nirvana we use phrases like this all the time to get positive messages across to victims when they are locked in a cycle of fear. It was our sugges-tion that the FMU's *Survivor's Handbook* should contain similar upbeat statements. *A journey of a thousand miles begins with a single step* is one that made it onto the cover of the handbook and perfectly describes the huge leap of faith so many of these victims need.

We are soon joined by Dr Rajat Mitra, the clinical psychologist who is the Director of Swanchetan. I am still in suspicious mode, half thinking to myself, 'Oh great, another Asian man who's bound to be full of his own importance. Am I really going to hear anything significant about honour-based violence from him?' At the back of my mind I'm assuming that he's the kind of professional who tries to talk victims into going back to their families. But Dr Mitra has a gentle face and manner and when he starts describing what his organisation does, it's clear that my preconceptions badly need adjusting.

He explains that when the rescued girls first arrive at the Swanchetan refuge, they are often completely dis-orientated. 'They do not know what is happening to them, or what to do, or where to go,' he tells me. 'Their minds have stopped working. They are not thinking clearly, they are not able to make any decisions. The analogy I often use is that they are like a deer caught in the headlights of a car. Some part of them wants every-thing to go back to the status quo, that somehow we should make everything all right again.' The second thing you see with these victims, he adds, is their over-riding concern for their personal safety. 'They're terrified. They feel their lives are in danger. If they're with small children, they feel that somehow they have to protect the lives of their children.'

This description exactly fits the young women we see at Karma Nirvana in the UK; it describes how I was, when I first ran away.

'And will they also experience depression?' I ask. 'Feelings of isolation?'

'At first what they experience is probably more like a feeling of numbness. The depression comes later, when the reality starts gaining on them as to what really has happened.'

Numb. That is precisely the word for what I felt for the first few months of my life after I ran away. I felt like a dead woman walking. I could see lots of people moving around the streets, but I couldn't hear them. Sometimes I even used to pinch myself, just to see if I could still feel. Hand on heart, this is the first time in my life I have met an Asian professional who has any idea what he is talking about in this area. But still there is a little part of me that remains cynical, that wants to test this man.

'Do you find these victims often harbour guilt?' I ask. 'Because they've gone against the wishes of the family?'

'This too is universal,' says Dr Mitra. 'It's the feeling that somehow I have brought this upon myself. If it wasn't for *me*, this situation would never have arisen in the first place. It is I who have shamed my family.'

Spot on. 'And what d'you think that can do to an individual?' I ask.

'That can make the person have very low self-esteem. Sometimes they are even suicidal. So the first thing we need to do is tell them they are not responsible for their situation. Perhaps we can connect them to a survivor of this sort of trauma who can say, "I've felt this too, I've been through exactly this same stage. So calm down and listen to me." Sometimes survivors are far better psychologists than we are.'

Whatever my reservations about Asian men, this guy is talking my language. Karma Nirvana was set up with survivors, its ongoing operation still depends on the time and effort put in voluntarily by survivors.

I decide I am ready to share my own story with him, to explain that I am not just a campaigner, but a survivor too. Despite everything he's said so far, I am still, at some level, finding it hard to unburden myself in front of an Asian man. But Dinesh was on my side. And now Dr Mitra listens with sympathy too (why on earth did I think that he wouldn't?).

I move on to describe how in due course I decided to put my experience to good use and found Karma Nirvana: how I started with a single phone in an unused room at the back of a women's centre and did my early promotion through keep-fit classes, an ideal way to reach vulnerable women in the Asian community without their husbands and fathers interfering; how I built up an organisation that within three years had lottery funding and now takes five thousand calls a year, over 30 per cent of which are from single victims of honour-based violence.

'Let me give you one telling statistic about the problem we face,' I say. 'You just talked about suicide. In the United Kingdom, British-born South Asian women between the ages of sixteen and twenty-four have a self-harm and suicide rate which is three or four times higher than the national average. Does that surprise you?'

'It doesn't,' Dr Mitra replies, in his mild, thoughtful voice. 'Because when we talk to the UK-born survivors over here, one of the things they share psychologically is that their families are still carrying the frozen values of when they left the Indian shores, forty, fifty years back. They have somehow preserved those values – and they go on making sure that women in particular live up to those values.'

This resonates powerfully with me. He is describing my parents and all the other Sikhs around them at home when I was growing up, trying to keep the Punjab alive in Derby. 'So why do they do this?' I ask.

'The families that left at that time arrived in the UK and were overwhelmed by the foreign culture. The only way they thought they could hold onto some sense of themselves was to retain the values with which they left.' Often, Dr Mitra continues, the way these values were upheld could be quite minute: starting with ways of structuring the day or what kind of clothes a child was going to be allowed to wear; moving on to who they were going to be allowed to talk to and how; right up to rules regarding dating and so on. 'When the children reach puberty, the parents feel they have to cut them off from the society around them. This is the time when we see this frozen values syndrome at the maximum, because these values are literally forced upon the person.'

'So why can't these girls just say "no", I'm not going to let you do this to me?' As I ask Dr Mitra this I realise I am still testing him. Because I know the answer; I just want to hear him tell me in his own words.

'They can't say "no", because "no" means death. It means I no longer love you. It means you are nobody. So the choice to say "no" does not exist with many of the families where you find these frozen values.'

That's quite a statement, but I know now that Dr Mitra understands this issue from the inside, emotionally, not just viewing it as a professional from the outside. In so many of these situations, a denial of the family's will is not possible for the victim; it's all or nothing: say 'yes' and stay or 'no' and leave.

'Frozen values are very subtle,' he continues. 'You won't see them in an overt way. Families won't talk about these things. They will say, "No, we are progressive, we have integrated, we have done this, we have done that." But in reality the whole situation is extremely controlling. The parents feel that this is the way they have to bring up their children, otherwise they have somehow failed.'

'Failed how?'

'When they left India for abroad, the one thing the

emigrants never thought would change was their family; that at least would continue as it had been at home. They never realised that things might be different, that their children might grow up in this new society with a different set of values; that they might see themselves as equals, and so on.'

'For someone like me, born in England, I don't know any other country. My father came over in the late 1950s . . .'

'And if you look at Punjab in the 1950s, the way he treated you is exactly the way he probably would have carried on at home . . .'

'How else to deal with a daughter wanting independence and the right to choose who she wants to marry?'

'Exactly. So not to carry on with what he knows means he has failed. Everything he stands for has failed.'

'In my experience, though, it wasn't so much my father as my mother. The perpetrators in my life were women. Is that typical?'

'It is often the case, yes. But I would also say that the women do what they do because of the pressure they face from men. Your mother is telling you to do certain things; one possible reason could be that she's also facing pressure from her husband, your father, stating this is how things should be.'

'Or the community? In England, the community features very large in how our Asian families behave. They worry about what their neighbours are going to say, their relatives, what people are going to say in the *gurdwara*, even in the next city.'

'But the pressure from the men contributes a great deal

towards that. Because otherwise this can just become a mother-blaming exercise. Men can say, "It's a woman who's doing all this. I didn't do it." Which absolves them of the responsibility.'

'As a survivor I have to make some sense of what happened to me for my own sanity. Because I can't explain how a father or mother could treat me like that. So part of my understanding, which makes me feel less angry, is for me to think that my parents were only doing what they knew. Not that that makes it right.'

'No. It doesn't. Your parents had a choice to do things differently. They had moved to a society where they were exposed to many more choices and options. And that's one of the reasons they went over there, to England, because they wanted to exercise those choices, compared to Punjab in the mid-1950s.'

As we chat on, I find Dr Mitra's observations revelatory. Most of all on this point about my parents having had choices. Nobody has put it quite like this to me before. They did indeed have choices: to come to the UK, and more important, once there, to integrate or not; they also, as he points out, could have chosen not to disown me in the way they did when I disobeyed them and ran away.

At the far end of the conference room on the left are two wooden doors. Now Dr Mitra stands to show us what lies behind them. One is a small toilet, very Asian, I notice, with a metal hose next to the toilet bowl rather than paper. The other is their secret refuge room. It has white walls, a green lino floor and a single bed with a floral duvet up against one wall. Next to it stands a TV on a wooden table.

There are bare shelves above. Green and yellow curtains are drawn against the sunshine outside.

I look at that sad television next to that sad little bed and I am transported immediately back to the room in Newcastle where I spent my first few weeks after I left home. That was a horrid place with cigarette burns in the dirty grey carpet. The only furniture apart from the bed was a rickety chest of drawers and two hard chairs. The kitchen was down lino stairs on the floor below: the place stank of old grease and only one ring worked on the cooker. Next to it was the dingy shared bathroom: always freezing because one of the windowpanes was smashed. Physically, it was in a much worse state than this little space, which at least is clean and tidy and safe. But emotionally, for a sixteen-year-old girl left on her own trying to work out what she has done, whether she's in the right, whose fault it is that she is in this predicament, whether she should turn against her instincts, swallow her pride and go back and submit to the will of her family – it's exactly the same.

'They put the television on,' says Dr Mitra, 'but they don't watch it.'

How well I understand that! Of course when I was in this situation I had Jassey there with me too. But after breakfast he would be up and off, out looking for work, and I would be left alone. I would spend the long days sitting there, trying to work out what I'd done and why I'd done it, curtains drawn against the world outside.

After a few weeks we were able to sign on for benefits and move to a cleaner place, but for me, wherever we went, it was still the same room. All I had to remind me of home were two photographs: one of my father and the other of my nephew, David, Ginda's eldest boy, aged about five at that time, whom I had often looked after and loved very much. Those and a panda bear that my sister Robina had made at school in needlework. She'd given it to me several birthdays before. Its ear was half-torn and one eye was hanging off.

What I didn't have was the warm, secure environment I had grown up with: Mum in the kitchen chopping vegetables for curry, Dad sitting opposite her at the wooden table sipping his tea before the night shift, Lucy watching telly in the living room – even Mum shouting at me to run down to the shop to get a bag of flour or a white loaf. Then at the weekends I was used to my sisters visiting, bringing my

My dad.

nephews and nieces with them, the arrival of numerous aunties with their busybody ways, my friends popping in.

When I finally summoned the courage to pick up the phone to my parents, my mother's reply was one line.

'In our eyes you're dead,' she told me. Then she hung up.

I sent my parents a letter, telling them how much I loved them, explaining that I didn't want to leave home, I just didn't want to marry the man they had chosen for me, but they still put the phone down on me.

Even three years after I'd run away, when my daughter Natasha was a baby and Jassey and I had moved to our own flat in the Asian area of Bradford, on the second floor in a row of old back-to-back brick houses on a steep hill, I still used to sit at the window and stare blankly out as the people went by outside. I had no milk in the house and the shop was less than a hundred yards from where we lived. But I had a fear of facing people, of the endless questions that the old Asian ladies, *bibis* as we called them, were bound to ask me. 'Where are you from?' 'Who is your father?' 'Where is your husband?' etc, etc. So I would wait for Jassey to come home and then ask him to go to the shop for me.

'You haven't had a cup of tea all day,' he would say when he got back. 'Why didn't you go to the shop?'

I used to try and explain that I had to psych myself up just to open the front door and leave the house. It wasn't a fear of being seen, it was more a fear of exposing the person I felt I had become because of what my family had done to me. Inside, I still felt that I was a bad person.

I pull myself out of my reverie and turn back to the

people around me: Dr Mitra, Dinesh from the High Commission, Tony. It is time to get professional again. Raise the issues I need to raise.

'So from here,' I say, 'these girls are handed over to the High Commission and returned to the UK. What kind of support do you think we should be giving them once they get back home?'

'I think the first thing,' Dr Mitra says, 'is to listen to their experiences, because they have been thrown into a completely different context and it has shaken their trust. Re-establishing trust for the victim is crucial. The second thing to get across to them is that they are now safe. It's important to say to them, "Even though you've had a traumatic experience that has been overwhelming, that has shaken your foundations, let's talk about that and deal with it, because you have overcome that and you are now a survivor."'

Exactly. But one of the things, I explain, that I have a huge issue with is what happens to these victims once they touch down in the UK. As I've already discussed with David and Dinesh, too often our Social Services and other agencies fail them and they end up back with their families. I am keen to get Dr Mitra's professional take on this; maybe he will give me some ammunition to help get to grips with this problem once I get home.

'So what do you think might happen if these girls return – or are returned – to their families? In psychological terms?'

Dr Mitra pauses for thought. 'The biggest thing relates to the girl's safety. If she goes back, her safety is compromised. Because by then, in many ways, she has already separated from her family. The belief will be that if the girl has not followed the dictates of elders, she is no longer a part of the family. "She might as well be dead for us" is a common saying. As a result, her relatives may feel they don't need to give her any support. Since she has brought shame and dishonour to the family, it may not be a bad idea if she is made to suffer even more. That suffering could push her to the point of death.'

'Suicide?'

'Yes. Or something that looks like suicide, but may not be.' Dr Mitra tells me of one shocking case Swanchetan had to deal with, where this was exactly what happened. A murder had been faked as suicide. 'So safety is the biggest issue here,' he concludes.

I sit back down on the bed. Dr Mitra has reaffirmed my instincts: that what happens to these girls on their return to the UK is crucial and may even be a matter of life and death. I am glad that Dinesh is here listening. This is an issue I am going to campaign about as soon as I get home.

But with Dr Mitra's talk of this case where murder was faked as suicide, I can't help but be thrown back to thinking about my sister Robina, and how her 'suicide' came about.

After the failure of her arranged marriage to Navtej, Robina went back to Derby with her little boy Sunny and lived with my parents for a while. During this time she met a man called Baldev, and the next thing I knew, they were going to get married. It was what Asian communities call 'a love match', and I remember being furiously jealous when I first heard about it. I had been disowned for running away with Jassey; now Robina was being allowed to do what she wanted in matters of the heart. Was it simply that Baldev was a *jatt*, like us? In any case, she was allowed to marry him and even given a full-on Asian wedding for her second time around. She wore a wedding sari heavily embroidered with gold. She had the red spot – the *bindi*, signifying her high caste – painted in the middle of her forehead. She was weighed down with gold bracelets and necklaces and of course the *nath*, the special gold wedding chain that runs across your face to your nose. Holy oil was poured on the doorstep of Dale Road before Robina went back into it, and all the women of the family cried as they made their formal goodbyes to her. (Not that, as a disowned sister, I was invited to the wedding, but Robina secretly gave me a copy of the video, which I still have.)

But sadly, despite the fact that this time she had decided her own destiny, Robina's second marriage was no happier than her first. In many ways it was harder for her the second time around because when she went to Mum and said, 'He's beating me up,' Mum would just say, 'Well, you chose him. It's a love marriage. You made your bed, now you'd better lie in it.'

Robina and I had been out of touch since I'd taken Lucy in, after the failure of her marriage; she rather took Mum's side on that. But desperation must have got to her, because she suddenly started ringing me out of the blue. Though she told me all was fine, from the tone of her voice I could sense otherwise. In the end, worried about her, and longing to see her again, too, I suggested a visit to her house in Leicester.

She and Baldev had a flashy enough place, complete with a built-in bar. But the evidence of their unhappy relationship was all around. There were holes in the wall of the lounge that had clearly been made by kicking. There was a smashed window on the ground floor and the door to the bathroom had been forced open. But Robina went on insisting that everything was fine.

The second time I went to visit Robina she came to meet me and Natasha at the bus station. I went to hug her and she flinched. 'Don't do that,' she said, looking down at six-year-old Sunny and shaking her head meaningfully. Later she explained that her ribs were bruised. She still refused to admit anything was wrong between her and Baldev, until finally she said, 'We just argue a lot.'

'So what are you going to do about it?' I said.

'There's nothing I can do.'

'Do Mum and Dad know?'

'Yes.'

'And they've done nothing?'

'No. What can they do? Mum keeps saying it was a love match.'

I told Robina she should leave Baldev. I offered her my place to live while she sorted herself out. But she wouldn't countenance that. 'That's easy enough for you to say,' she said. 'You don't have to consider Mum and Dad and what people might think. I couldn't do that to them. They're only just now recovering from what happened when you ran away. Mum's just beginning to hold her head up in the *gurdwara*, people who've cut her off for years are starting to talk to her. If I left Baldev the shame would kill them.'

A fortnight later she was dead. She had, her husband said, set fire to herself and burnt to death in the bedroom of their home. The story Baldev told us was that Robina poured paraffin on her clothes while they were arguing, then put a match to herself before he could stop her. By the time the ambulance arrived she had suffered 90 per cent burns. She was so disfigured that when she was laid out before her funeral in a casket, against all our traditions it was closed. Instead they put a photograph of her on top.

Nobody apart from Baldev knows exactly what happened that day, but my take on it was that she was driven to suicide. Shortly before she died I got a very strange call from her. She said, 'I need you to do something for me.'

'Of course, Robina,' I replied, 'Are you leaving him? D'you want to come and stay here?'

'You know I can't leave him,' she said. Then, 'I'd like you to contact Sunny's father.'

'Why me?' I asked. 'Why can't you do it?'

'I've tried to ring him,' she told me, 'but when he answers and I hear his voice I just freeze up. I can't bring myself to speak to him. Will you do it for me?'

'Why now all of a sudden?'

'I want Sunny to know his father. If anything happens to me I want him to know his real father.'

'Why are you saying this, Robina?'

'Just promise me you'll do it,' she replied. It was the last conversation I had with her.

I managed to get the original cause of death, suicide, changed in an inquest to an open verdict. I'm sorry we didn't get more than that. I never thought it was murder, but there are many unanswered questions about that day. If Baldev was in the house when this self-immolation happened, which he was, why didn't he act quicker to stop it? Robina's whole body was on fire and she suffered 90 per cent burns. He hardly had any. Surely if someone was burning to death in front of you you'd jump in and try and do something?

The day Robina died was her and Baldev's anniversary. It came out in the inquest that she had just found out that Baldev was having an affair. The forensic scientist found clear evidence that they had been fighting: a coffee table was on its side, a plate that had hung on the wall lay smashed on the floor, there was a hole in the lounge door, in addition to the dents I'd already seen in the walls. Six weeks after Robina's death Baldev went to live with the woman he'd been having the affair with.

Nowadays you can prosecute for psychological harassment. It seems to me that was closer to the case than suicide. Whatever happened, the bottom line was that Robina was only in the situation she was because she feared the shame that she would bring on her family if she tried to get out of it.

After such a horrific thing had happened, I was misguided enough to think that my family might find it in their hearts to allow me back. But no. Robina's death seemed only to reinforce my rejection. When I turned up to join the mourners at Mum and Dad's house, my sisters stood up as one, wrapped their white scarves around their heads and walked out. I was then told to stay away from the funeral. I ignored that, Robina had always been the sister I was closest to and

I wasn't going to let them stop me being there. But for me it was a turning point: I had to accept that, whatever happened, my family were never going to change. If there was going to be any forgiveness it was going to have to come from me.

When I share the outline of this story with Dr Mitra, he is understanding but not surprised. He has been close to too many cases of honour-based abuse for that. He assures me that my family's continuing rejection is not unusual. Forgiveness, he says, usually comes, if at all, very late for the survivor, both in terms of the family forgiving the victim and the victim forgiving the family. There was even one case, he tells me, where the survivor said, after many years, that the perpetrators had asked for forgiveness and she was uncertain what she should do about it. 'I remember how she talked about it to me. She said, "I don't think I can forgive my mother for what she did, because the person who could have forgiven her is dead. I'm a new person today."'

This is fascinating. When I've interviewed survivors, they often talk about a 'person' who was abused, whom they feel sorry for – when that person is in fact them. I remember one case that I was involved with in my role as an expert court adviser where the victim said, 'I feel sorry for that girl whose father forced the Koran under her nose and made her swear that she would never go on Facebook again. The girl that did that should be ashamed of herself.' She was talking about herself.

As for me, perhaps what Dr Mitra has made me understand, deep in the suburbs of Delhi on this warm

November afternoon, is what I really feel about my family after all these years. That I have changed so much that I am no longer the person who sat in those rooms in Newcastle and Bradford with the curtains drawn day after day. Perhaps I can say, along with this other survivor Dr Mitra has talked about, that the person who could have forgiven them all is dead.

4

Stuck in Delhi's dense rush-hour traffic on the way back to the guest house I'm still thinking about my family. For years after I was disowned by my parents I tried with all of them for some kind of reconciliation. But it didn't happen. Then, finally, in the two years after Robina's death, when Mum was diagnosed with bowel cancer and became a shadow of her former self, I got back on some kind of speaking terms with her and my father. Together, in secret, Mum and I instigated the inquest into Robina's suicide and then when Mum was sick, I took to visiting her regularly, bathing her and caring for her in her last days.

But my sisters continued to stay aloof from me, blowing hot and cold, recognising me only when it suited them. At important family occasions, like weddings and funerals, I was either not invited or blanked. This continuing rejection led to some absurd situations. Sometimes when I was visiting my mother when she was terminally ill, one of my sisters would turn up at the house without warning and I would have to rush upstairs and hide in a bedroom or make a sharp exit through the back garden. You might wonder why I put up with such humiliation, but I did, terrified that if I didn't go along with what Mum saw as right, I would lose the relationship I had just recovered with her and Dad.

Even at my mother's deathbed my sisters appeared to pretend I wasn't there, as I stood at the head of the bed holding the frail old fingers of her hand. When that hand went limp, and Mum had taken her last breath, there was no sharing of the grief for me. My sisters cried and hugged each other and I was left standing. They left the hospital together in a group, and I had to make my way home alone.

It's ironic to think that when I first ran away, hiding in that grim bedsit in Newcastle, I had imagined that it was my sisters who would support me. Mum and Dad's harsh reaction – telling me I was dead in their eyes, then putting the phone down whenever I rang up – had been shocking but at some level expected, even understood. But realising my siblings were going to do the same was, if anything, worse.

My younger sister Lucy was the first of them to give me hope that one day we might resume normal relations. In the first two years after I'd run away, she had at least spoken to me when I called, even if it was not the straightforward friendly voice I'd been used to at home. 'Don't you realise what you've done to us?' she hissed down the phone. 'How difficult it is for Gin? What they're saying in the *gurdwara*?' It was Lucy who told me that other women from the local Sikh community were spitting at Mum in the street.

After two years, Lucy was the first to speak to me

properly on the phone and fill me in, on the quiet, on family news. Then she met up with me that time in Derby's Markeaton Park, when she looked so smart and free with her short bob and fashionable Western skirt. She visited me and Jassey in our Bradford flat, kept in touch from Germany after she got married, then came and lived with us when she left her husband. For a while that summer of 1988 we were back to being as close as we'd ever been, going out to pubs and clubs together and having a great time.

But later, when she'd picked herself up and was back living and working in Derby, she went cool on me again. She had forged a strong relationship with Ginda at that point, and Ginda had not been reconciled to me. Little by little I began to realise that the pair of them were attending the kinds of family weddings and occasions I would never be allowed to go to. Then, when I set up Karma Nirvana, Lucy stopped talking to me entirely. It became embarrassing, because she was working as a receptionist at the doctors where I was registered. I would walk into the surgery, go up to the counter and say my name, and Lucy would roll her eyes and get somebody else to come and speak to me. In the end I had to change doctors. I thought, 'I'm not going to come in here with my children if she's going to behave like this.'

The summer after my father died, Lucy arrived on my doorstep unannounced again. Things had gone wrong for her and she had nowhere else to go. She had wanted to stay with Ginda, but Shinda had never really forgiven her for running away from his nephew, so that wasn't an option.

So I took her in. But our relationship fell apart again after that. And when *Shame* came out, in 2007, Lucy was highly critical of what I'd written, and things deteriorated even further.

Robina was the other sister I was very close to when I was growing up. When Lucy came to visit me for the first time in Bradford, Robina turned up soon after, bringing Sunny, her little boy. Her first marriage had failed, and as she filled me in on that unhappy story I felt once again as intimate with her as I had before I'd left. But then, when she married Baldev with the blessing of my parents and there was that big family celebration, I was not invited. Hot, cold; hot, cold. When I married Jassey, shortly after that, Robina was there for me again: taking a big part in helping with the preparations, going round the Asian shops to buy my maroon wedding sari, lending me the special jewellery I couldn't afford, bracelets and necklaces and even the *nath* she had worn herself. She was there with Lucy on my wedding day. She came to visit me when Natasha was born and encouraged my mother to come and visit too. But then when Lucy left her husband and came to live with me, and my mother refused to talk to me, Robina went quiet on me too. It was only when her second marriage was in serious trouble that our relationship resumed. She never explained why she'd been out of touch, or even mentioned it. Shortly after that she was dead.

My relationship with Yasmin has been the simplest of all. Since I ran away we have never spoken. At all. Even at funerals we've barely made eye contact.

Ginda, though, has been different – another hot and cold affair. For years after I ran away she didn't speak to me at all. Then, when I moved back to Derby in 1990, after Robina's death, and was calling in on Mum on the quiet, Ginda would sometimes be there at Dale Road. She was going through a rough patch with Shinda and staying with Mum and Dad for a while. At that point she would talk to me. And I was able to see her two children again, David and Sereena, which was wonderful for me after such a long break. They were now teenagers, not the naughty little children I had known before I ran away. We even went to the seaside together, taking all our kids for a day out at Skegness. We paddled in the water and had fish and chips; it was lovely, for a moment, almost back to where we'd been when I was a child.

But then, when she went back to Shinda, Ginda's behaviour changed. She blanked me completely in the street one time when I was out doing my Saturday shopping. Then, much later, after Dad died, and I moved to a big house in Derby, I was back in favour for a while. 'OK,' she said to me, 'now you are living in a respectable area. You've not got a husband, but if your neighbours ask, you can just say he works away from home.'

There was an ulterior motive for this sudden friendliness, because I was looking after Robina's teenaged son Sunny at this time. Dad had left him our parents' house in his will, and Ginda had been furious about that. She felt the house should have been shared among the family and she thought that I might be able to talk Sunny into agreeing to change the will to favour all of us.

'He listens to you,' she said. 'Get round him.' She used the Punjabi word *mudjiati,* which means, work on him, persuade him. 'Get him to divide the house between us all.' I got the impression that, if I succeeded, then I could be fully part of the family again.

I was shocked. Dad had made it clear who he was leaving his money to, and that was that. I wasn't going to be party to any emotional blackmail of Sunny; or me, for that matter.

'Absolutely not,' I replied. 'No way are we going to go against what Dad wanted.'

Ginda was furious. She told me that Lucy and all my other sisters thought the same way as her and that I should support them. Here we are, I thought, back at square one.

For me, the point of no return with my sisters came when *Shame* was published. Before that I had kept trying to be reconciled with them all, kept trying to be part of the family. But I knew that in publishing *Shame*, giving my side of this story, the door would be completely closed. At one level this was quite healing for me. I was taking charge. I was saying, finally, 'OK, enough hot and cold, I just want out of this. For ever.' I even made a will stipulating that I didn't want any of my family at my funeral. I just couldn't continue in this position of wanting something that wasn't ever going to be given.

Ever since I left home all those years before, any relationship I'd had with them had always been on their terms. I use the analogy that going into my family's house was like walking into a house on fire. When I walked out I would always be burnt to some degree. I simply never knew what I was going to be faced with. They threw me scraps from time to time, but then they would withdraw. I just got to the point where I thought, 'You are not going to do this to me any more.'

I was right about *Shame*. They were furious. I even had a death threat from one of my brother Balbir's daughters. I heard about it from a colleague. She told me that she had been out with a group of friends that included my niece, who had been saying that what I had written degraded her grandmother and grandfather's memory; that she was going to have me killed and Natasha as well. At one level this seemed ridiculous, but then, as I know all too well from my work with Karma Nirvana, nobody can afford to be complacent in this area. I decided to take her threat seriously. I called the police and they went round to Dawn's house and tried to caution her daughter. My niece wouldn't come to the door and Dawn made a big scene so in the end they had to escort the girl to the police station. The police then contacted me. 'What d'you want to do?' they said. 'She's not denying her threats, but this is an eighteen-year-old girl doing her A-levels. If she gets a formal caution it's going to be on her record for a long time.' In the end I told them to leave it, but not before making sure the police pointed out to her that I could have taken things further.

The tensions continue. I no longer expect any different. My resolution was tested the other day when my older sister Prakash got in touch out of the blue. She phoned the Karma Nirvana office but didn't introduce herself as my sister. She asked to speak to me. My colleague Shazia took the call and asked who was calling and what it was about. This woman said it was private, so Shazia asked, as always when fielding my calls, whether she could just give her a brief idea. The woman wouldn't say, but in the end she gave her name and number. 'She'll know who I am,' she said. 'Say it's Prakash from Slough.'

So Shazia came over to me and told me she'd had this very strange call from a woman called Prakash from Slough. I had an idea it was my sister, so I phoned her son Ranjit to check the number. (For reasons I'll go into later, Ranjit, who has been disowned, is the one member of the extended family I am in touch with.) Sure enough, it was Prakash's number. So I left it. She called every day for five days. In the end I rang Ranjit again. 'Have you any idea why she might be trying to contact me?' I asked. He thought it was probably something to do with his brother, who was in trouble with the police. He had got high on drink or drugs and stabbed his wife. Ranjit's guess was that Prakash had seen me on television and thought I might have influence or contacts, might be able to help.

Then Prakash's husband rang, asking to speak to me urgently. It was a family matter, he said. Prakash had never said she was my sister, but now it was 'a family matter'. I said to Shazia, 'Tell my sister the next time she rings that you have passed the message on to me, that you have told me her name is Prakash, but Jasvinder has no idea who you are.' Which is what Shazia did. Prakash said 'Oh' and put the phone down. That was it.

My reaction was harsh, I know. After years of rejection I had moved on. A few years ago I would have run to the phone like a dog with my tail wagging if I'd thought it was someone from my family getting in contact. But not now, no, even though all my colleagues at Karma Nirvana were telling me this was my big opportunity for a reconciliation.

It's not just about me. The way my sisters have treated my children, blanking them in the street, not recognising them, is unforgiveable. Worse than that, they have robbed them of their heritage, their future with their family. Children don't ask to be born. They could have treated them so differently.

My daughter Natasha is a very forgiving person; she will say it's OK, she doesn't mind – but I'm sure she feels it too. Being cut off like that. From the people who should be her family.

When we finally make it back to the guest house, Tony and I share a vegetarian curry before we turn in. I am in a contemplative mood, thinking over the day, in particular what Dr Mitra said at the end about forgiveness. That sometimes survivors can't forgive their families, because the person who could have forgiven them no longer exists. I have not heard it put that way before, and it resonates so strongly with me. It makes me realise that, deep down, despite all the self-help books I've read, and all that I've told myself over the years, I haven't really forgiven them. I thought I had, because I so badly wanted to move on. But now I realise that: a) I haven't and b) more importantly, I don't need to.

There was that other thing Dr Mitra said, too, just before

we went into the refuge room: that it was my parents' choice to go to the UK, not mine. If they didn't want to go to a culture that puts a value on individual liberty, they didn't have to. It was their choice not to integrate and their choice, subsequently, to disown me.

5

When I woke this morning I decided to dress in Asian clothes. Before I left for this journey, Anup's mother Neelam lent me an Asian wardrobe, as I gave up wearing Asian suits and saris long ago, when I left home. After my rejection, the dress of my mother and her community became for me a symbol of the oppression I'd experienced. I decided I would only ever put it on at a time and a place of my choosing.

So I wasn't sure quite what I was going to wear on this trip. Of course I want to respect the Indian culture; on the other hand I am British-born and raised. At Natasha's suggestion, I agreed to spend a day in Bradford looking round the Asian shops. Maybe, I thought, I'd get myself a couple of suits and saris, just in case. But when I got to Anup's house to pick up Natasha, Neelam insisted I look through her wardrobe. 'You must take some Asian clothes,' she said, as she handed me a welcoming glass of *chai*. 'Apart from anything else, they're so comfortable in that climate. Shall we go upstairs because I've got a few things I've picked out for you.'

I thought she might have a couple of outfits for me to try on, but when we got up to her room, the bed was covered with *salwar kameez* and saris in every colour under the sun. 'Try this! Take this!' Neelam was saying, as I paced up and down in front of the mirror, enjoying the soft feel of the clothes and liking the look of them, but wondering whether I could really bring myself to wear any of them.

'You look great, Mum,' Natasha said, as Neelam reached up to the top of the wardrobe and started bringing down bag after bag, opening them and holding the clothes up

Me with Anup's mother.

against me. She even wanted me to take the beautiful sari her husband had given her as an anniversary present. 'Please,' she said, 'just in case you have to go to an occasion. You will look beautiful in it.'

I refused the sari and a load of jewellery Neelam wanted me to take, too, but I still ended up with a suit for every day of the week. Neelam even lent me a huge black suitcase to put them all in. I felt a little embarrassed by the contrast, to be honest, because we were both Asian women of the same age and yet I didn't possess a single Asian outfit. I did once have a few suits, and a couple of saris too, but I threw them all out the day that Ginda came to my house in Warwick Avenue and asked me to try and persuade Sunny to change my father's will. Enough is enough, I thought. I stuck them in a black bin bag and dropped them off at Oxfam.

Now that I'm here, in India, I'm so glad I brought that suitcase. I'm starting to feel so much more relaxed about embracing this culture than I ever imagined was possible. For a start, it feels good to be among so many Asian people. However British I am by birth and education, in the UK I also feel part of a minority. Here, even though I'm a foreigner, in some ways I don't feel like one. I look the same as everyone else. It's strangely reassuring.

There is also the language. At home we spoke Punjabi, so I'm fluent in it, even though I rarely get a chance to use it these days so it's a bit rusty. Here in Delhi the predominant language is Hindi, but they still understand Punjabi. At this guest house where we're staying, there are two guys who look after the place and cook the wonderful breakfasts and vegetable curries that we've been eating in the evening. They are from Bengal, so they pronounce words differently, but we still have an understanding. They see I'm not white English, so they have a curiosity about me. Regardless of where I'm from, there is a commonality about us. We share the fact that we have a connection with India. They may have been born here, but then so was my father. I have never felt that connection in England. If I were in Southall, for example, and I was surrounded by Sikhs, I wouldn't feel part of Southall. But here in India, I do feel part of it all.

Maybe this sense of fitting in is also because I feel anonymous here. In the UK, if you're in an Asian area, people always want to know where you're from, just as they did when I was nursing Natasha in that little flat in Bradford. Pakistani Muslims will ask Punjabi Sikhs, and vice versa. They can't help themselves. Where have you come from? Is that where your parents live? Who's your father? Mother? And where do *they* come from? On it goes. Straight away if you're Asian in the UK you are somebody. Other Asians want to know where you fit in. Whereas here you're just one of the crowd.

So today I want to take that process of losing my identity in the crowd one stage further. From Neelam's big suitcase I pick out a pair of pale yellow trousers; over that I put a thin *kameez* which has stripes of a pale purply-grey, overprinted with purple floral patterns. Over that I sling a fawn-orange woollen *dupatta* or shawl. Suddenly I am a proper Asian. It feels good, easy, almost like a second skin.

* * *

David and Dinesh have been working hard on my behalf. Before we leave Delhi to go north, they are keen that I see another refuge, this one run by a group who call themselves the Love Commandos. This is a Delhi-based outfit that was recently formed to help couples in India who are attempting to have 'love marriages', who face anything from the obstruction of their families through to the sentence of an 'honour killing' handed down by a *khap panchayat* (village council).

This is one step beyond the problems encountered by the girls from the UK who are brought to India; but it is this same retrograde world that our British girls are often taken back to – the rural villages where groups of elders still sit in judgement on couples that attempt to marry across caste. This, more importantly, is the context, providing the background and to some extent the justification for what goes on in the UK. My mother's objection to my marriage to Jassey, for example, was based largely on the fact that he was from a lower caste – the *chamars*, once known as the untouchables, while my family were *jatts*, the higher, land-owning caste. As my daughter Lisa, well removed from these cruel anachronisms, once said, 'What does this make me – a half-caste?'

Dr Mitra spoke yesterday about the 'frozen values' of the families who emigrated to the UK in the 1950s and 60s. His analysis struck a chord with me, and in my view he is right about British Asians who cling to old values and customs that have no relevance whatever to the world around them. But this doesn't mean that India has meanwhile moved on in its attitude to forced marriage and honour killings. A glance through the Indian newspapers stacked up in the lounge of our little guest house reveals how these issues, particularly in the northern states of India, are still very much alive. Among the headlines that speak of an altogether contemporary India – TWEETS A RUNNING COMMENTARY ON PARLIAMENT SPEECH; STANDING ORDERS TO BE DIGITALISED; BOLLYWOOD CAN WAIT – ABIDA PARVEEN are others that chill the blood.

COUPLE MURDERED FOR 'HONOUR' IN PUNJAB

FEROZEPUR: In another case of 'honour killing', a young couple of Scheduled Caste community was murdered allegedly by the girl's mother with the help of her two relatives. The girl, identified as Puja (17), and her young lover Rakesh (18), both residents of Nurpur Sethan village near Ferozepur, had been in love for the past two years.

The bodies of the victims were found lying in a pool of blood in a field in Kotwal village on Monday. The bodies were spotted by a farmer, who was irrigating his farm, adjacent to the field where the dead were lying.

Police sources said Rakesh and Puja were in a relationship. As the family members were resisting their relationship, both ran away from their homes about one and a half months ago. However, both were brought back to Nurpur Sethan village after they were persuaded by their family members and other kin. After returning to the village, Puja was sent to her cousin's place at Kotwal village.

According to sources, Rakesh was reportedly called to Kotwal village by Puja's mother, where he was allegedly murdered with a sharp-edged weapon by Parminder Kaur,

Billa (girl's uncle) and one unidentified person. When Puja came to know about the killing of her lover, she threatened that she would report the matter to the police, following which the trio also killed Puja. Later, her body was thrown in the fields of Tehal Singh.

Though no villager is willing to talk on the issue, the police claimed that it was clearly a case of honour killing.[1]

The Love Commandos refuge that we are visiting is in a district of Delhi called Paharganj, close to the main New Delhi Railway Station, which is frequented by backpackers and tourists on a low budget. The streets are narrow and muddy, awash with grey puddles. Mopeds and motorcycles, horns blaring, race through the jostle of pedestrians, pedal-cycle rickshaws, carts pulled by horse or human. A fruit stall stacked with peaches and bananas stands by a cart covered with boxes of white eggs, a greasy black frying pan lying ready to make omelettes on one side. Behind are shop fronts crowded with shiny snack packets, electrical items, mobile phones, brightly coloured garments. Several windows are hung with looped strings of orange chrysanthemums. Above, a thick tangle of electrical and telephone wires, some held up by rope, criss-crosses among the hotel and shop signs. Sahara Guest House, Le Roi, Gold Inn, Sahil Saloon, Hotel Assam, Queen Palace – Always At Your Service.

A man walks by pushing a bicycle from which fly several colourful bunches of children's balloons. A dark brown

---

[1] *The Times of India* 9.11.10

pony is led past, its head down, its back laden. Scrawny dogs roam idly among the roadside rubbish.

The refuge is in a ramshackle two-storey house in a backstreet crowded with windows and balconies. In the front room of one dwelling a man in a turquoise T-shirt and loose trousers with a gold-orange cummerbund around his waist, is washing down a fine white stallion. As Tony and I approach the refuge, I am aware of people watching from unlikely corners: an old man with a long white beard squatting on a doorstep, two women in orange saris sitting on a low roof; a gaggle of bright-eyed children holding hands next to two dogs asleep in the shade.

Through the low front door is a narrow kitchen, where a plate of dried peas and chopped onion sits on top of a colander on a marble sideboard. Beyond another door are two tiny rooms, each just big enough for a double bed. A fluorescent strip light runs between exposed beams. Next to this is a white plastic fan, dirty and immobile. There is a glass cabinet along one wall, stuffed full of junk: old books, videos, battered toys. On an overhead shelf is a mass of curled, yellowing papers and a mini plastic palm tree. The walls are painted a bright blue. On the beds are thick patterned quilts, those same exotic *rajai* that my mother used to bring back from her trips to India when I was a child.

A couple of young men are hanging around the kitchen area. Through in the main bedroom we meet Mr Harsh Malhotra, a squat figure with chubby features and a thick dark moustache, who wears a pristine and slightly shiny white *salwar kameez*. He is one of the founders of the Love

Commandos. More Asian men, actively involved in the fight against honour-based violence! I continue to be surprised and impressed.

Mr Malhotra and I sit, rather awkwardly, on the double bed in the inner room. One of the young men brings us *chai*, in little glass cups on a shiny black tray. The Love Commandos developed, Mr Malhotra explains, from a group called the Valentine's Day Peace Commandos, who started nine years ago with the aim of countering the harassment that couples out in public receive on Valentine's Day, when they take part in the annual 'Love Birds' march, asserting their right to fall in love with whoever they choose. At that time the Peace Commandos launched a campaign with the slogan '*Nirbhay hoka manao Valentine's Day*' ('Celebrate Valentine's Day Without Fear') and armed themselves with sticks and chilli powder sprays to chase away the Hindu fundamentalists who carry out these attacks.

Then on Valentine's Day 2010 the Love Commandos were formed, initially as a gesture in support of a couple who had tried unsuccessfully to get married six times, but had been prevented as they came from different castes. The new group succeeded in getting the couple married, then in finding them jobs and a home well away from the families who had been trying to stop them.

On 7 July 2010, after an alarming spate of honour killings across the north of India, the Love Commandos decided to launch a helpline. They were immediately overwhelmed with calls, Mr Malhotra tells me. Fortunately volunteers soon materialised to help: to man phones, offer advice and provide refuge accommodation.

In the first instance, the Love Commandos will counsel a distressed couple over the phone. If a situation is considered to be serious, a local team will be sent out to the area in question, and the Love Commandos will try and get the police involved in mediation with the family, and if that doesn't work, in protecting the couple. This isn't always easy, as the police often take the side of the relatives rather than the couple and generally insist on continuing mediation rather than providing straightforward protection.

In some places, the authorities actively support the status quo. In the province of Haryana, for example, between Delhi and the Punjab, the state government recently issued a statement saying that they respected the village elders who form *khap panchayats* and would not try to undermine their position. Meanwhile the problem is serious and ongoing. In Punjab province alone, there have been 102 honour killings in the last year.

The Love Commandos started, Mr Malhotra continues, with a handful of volunteers. They now have 2000 actively involved, with another 200,000 pending membership. They have five centres in Delhi, and others in the states of Punjab, Maharashtra, Andhra Pradesh and Uttar Pradesh. They have 12 helplines and have already organised 6000 inter-caste love marriages across India, as well as counselling thousands of people. These are extraordinary statistics, but the sincerity of Mr Harsh Malhotra and his commitment to the cause is tangible and clear.

When we've finished our tea we are joined by the young couple who are currently using the refuge. Sanjay is a fit looking guy, smartly turned out in an ironed cotton shirt over grey jeans. He sits in a moulded plastic chair beside the bed, his long legs stretched out towards me. His partner Arti squats cross-legged on the bed next to me, in a long purple skirt, her head and shoulders wrapped in a green shawl with white spots. She is wide-eyed and looks terrified; I immediately find myself thinking of Dr Mitra's analogy of a deer caught in the headlights. Arti is only eighteen, Sanjay explains, but her mother has already sold her in marriage three times. In each case her mother gave her husband permission to beat her if she didn't conform to his wishes. Each time she escaped and returned home, only for her mother to marry her off again; her mother only cares about the money, Sanjay says, that she could get from each union.

Sanjay has known Arti since she was a young teenager. They love each other. Eventually he managed to save 6000 rupees and pay off her mother, who promised him he could now marry her. But then, when he had handed over the money to her, she sent a group of men to beat him up. In desperation, Arti ran away and Sanjay joined her. They contacted the Love Commandos and escaped to Delhi. The Love Commandos tried to mediate with the family, but when the police arrived on the scene, they took the side of the family. The marriage clearly wasn't going to happen. So the couple escaped again, and now they are in hiding here, while the Love Commandos make an application through the courts for a protection order.

I listen to their case with great sympathy, but I'm afraid to say I am not surprised by what they have told me. I have heard so many similar stories back home; indeed, sitting on this tatty double bed opposite this pair takes me back to the early days of Karma Nirvana, when I would offer advice to frightened girls in backstreet refuges in the UK. Over here at least the issue is out in the open, it is widely acknowledged and reported. Our problem at home is that many people don't believe that such things are going on. How many times have I heard the voices of otherwise switched-on professionals in the UK saying, 'Surely this can't be happening? You *what*? She's being forced to marry her *what*? It was arranged at her birth?' The dreadful cases I recount from personal experience in my second book, *Daughters of Shame*, are just a selection of what I've heard over the years and are the ones I've been allowed to tell.

Now I hold Arti's hand and wish them both luck. Arti smiles, and for just a moment, the petrified look in her eyes is replaced by something gentler. I can only pray that this calmness is going to be something she gets used to in her abused young life; that the pair of them are going to be all right, and not end up as yet another page five headline in *The Times of India*.

Mr Malhotra invites us back to his house a couple of streets away. We climb up narrow stairs to a roof terrace with a fine view out over the rooftops of central Delhi: a jumble of TV aerials, big black plastic water tanks, a mobile phone mast, a row of orange flowerpots, a couple of white plastic office chairs stranded on a roof.

We talk some more about the role of the police. Mr Malhotra's experience of the authorities is not as benign as

Dinesh's. Hardly surprising perhaps, as with the High Commission, the police not only have a protocol in place, they are dealing with foreign nationals. With their own domestic cases, Mr Malhotra tells me, Sanjay and Arti's story is not atypical. All too often the police turn a blind eye or take the family's side. The junior officers are, in his experience, often the worst.

I decide that the time has come to tell Mr Malhotra my own story. Partly because I want him to know that I have personal experience of the kind of injustices he and I are campaigning against; partly, too, because once again I want to test the water. What will another Asian man, very different again from Dinesh and Dr Mitra, make of what happened to me? When I've finished, I'm happy to say, he is genuinely taken aback. 'For whose honour are your family not talking to you?' he asks. He is equally shocked when I tell him that we have honour killings in the UK too. Just in this last week, the tragic case of Banaz Mahmod, strangled with a bootlace for leaving an unhappy arranged marriage to be with the man she loved, was finally put to rest when her murderers, extradited from Iraq, were sentenced to life imprisonment. (I am proud to say I had a hand in helping that extradition, chivvying our representatives in both the House of Commons and the Lords until action was taken.) I also tell him about Rukhsana Naz, Nuziat Khan, Heshu Yones, Anita Ghinda, Samaira Nazir and all the others. Mr Malhotra thought that the UK was a progressive and democratic society.

Three times he asks me if I was really born in England.

Because of what happened to me, he can't believe I was. 'Are you sure you were?' he asks.

'Of course I'm sure! And my sisters were as well.'

He is keen to reassure me that in his eyes I have nothing to be ashamed of – unlike my family. There is no way I did anything wrong in following the path I chose. 'Just because you give birth to a child,' he says, 'it doesn't give you the right to kill it.'

I am so encouraged by these Asian men who are working so actively in this area: Dinesh Kumar, Dr Mitra and now Mr Harsh Malhotra. I realise too that they are all from the city, all progressive members of this vast and complex society that is modern India. I am not sure what kind of men I am going to find in the rural area I am headed to all too soon but my instincts tell me they will not be like these.

On our way back to our guest house Tony and I stop at a bar in Connaught Place, the big circle of white Georgian-style buildings at the very centre of Delhi. Designed and built by the British architect Sir Edwin Lutyens, it was modelled, apparently, after the Royal Crescent in Bath. Its British heritage is all too obvious, though now the elegant white pillars are hung with strings of bright light bulbs and the neon signs below the arched windows advertise businesses from a very different era than the end of Empire.

The bar is cool and contemporary with funky waiters in blue shirts and soft green caps. It's Happy Hour and 'Sex on the Beach' is just one of the cocktails on offer. The long shared wooden tables are crowded with young people of both sexes having a good time. Sitting in here, the idea that this is still a country where people can be harassed to the point of death for trying to form relationships based on love seems utterly unlikely.

6

I realised last night, turning things over in my mind after meeting Dr Mitra, that I had never really forgiven my parents or my siblings in England. But my oldest sister Bachanu is not contaminated by the way the others have treated me over the years. She has never met me, never known me, never had a chance either to accept me or reject me. My children and I could still have a relationship with her. She could be a way back to us having some sort of wider family.

Back in my room at the guest house, I take the photograph I have of her from the sheaf at the top of my suitcase. It's not very big, six inches by four, but it's the only one I have. My sister stands in an open, covered area, grinning, holding a toddler in blue shorts. She wears a white silk *salwar kameez* with turquoise trousers, a long pink shawl over her head and neck. Next to her is another woman in a pale grey outfit with a purple shawl. Behind them lies a blue Ford tractor (I think as a family we may have contributed to that). At this size it's hard to read Bachanu's expression, but she looks nice: warm, straightforward, practical. The photo is a colour one, but I've no idea when it was taken.

I really don't know what will happen when we get to Kang Sabhu, but I'm praying that Bachanu will open her arms and welcome me. That would make up for such a lot of lost time. Just this one person. In my mind's eye I imagine it as a fairy tale meeting, where we are both so pleased to see each other. There are tears of joy, hugs, and talk of how I have grown (for in this fantasy she knows all about me, has pictures of me when I was smaller). Then reality hits me and I have an awful sinking feeling. What stories has she been told about me? What if she views me as dishonourable? What if she doesn't want to see me? What if she slams the door in my face, then gets others to hunt me down and deal with me?

Until I made my trip, this was the only photograph that I had of my sister Bachanu (right).

I have, over the years, got used to a level of aggression and risk in relation to the work I do. On some occasions it's no more than a hostile heckler, like the Sikh man who stood up recently at a talk I was giving in Nottingham about honour killings and asked whether I regarded myself as honourable. He seemed polite enough, but my antennae were twitching, and as I looked out over the audience, I wondered what on earth might be coming next.

'If you are asking, if I have honour,' I said, 'then yes, I do have honour.'

'Is it honourable then for a woman to have an affair when she has a wonderful husband? To run off and have an affair like a dirty animal.'

I was gobsmacked but I wasn't going to let him see that, or anyone else in the room.

'First of all,' I said, 'let's be clear here. You're asking me if it's honourable to have an affair. Are you talking about me?'

He wouldn't answer that, though he clearly was.

'Just tell me,' he repeated, 'is it honourable for a woman to have an affair?'

I said, 'Right, I'll answer this for you. First of all I do believe you *are* talking about me. Yes, I chose to tell the world in my book *Shame* that I did have an affair when I was 21, and yes, at the time I was married. Can I make this point – I didn't have to tell the world that. You didn't have to know that. I chose to tell you that. The reason I chose to tell you is to show you that I'm a human being. I ran away from home as a naive fifteen-year-old girl. I had never had a relationship in my life. I don't personally find it acceptable to have an affair and today I would never do that, but I was being honest about what happened. It's called life experience. If you are asking me, have I learnt from that today, yes I have. Do I have honour? Yes, I do. Absolutely.'

I'm glad to say on that occasion the audience broke into spontaneous supportive applause. The man had clearly been planning his verbal attack though, because afterwards he came up to one of my colleagues as I was signing books and demanded he accept a letter on my behalf. I didn't bother reading it; life's too short and I don't need to upset myself. The guy actually phoned Karma Nirvana a couple of days later wanting to know whether I'd read his stupid letter. My colleague Shazia was her usual professional self, telling him it had been passed on to me and doubtless I would get to it in due course.

'I bet she has time to sit in the pub,' he said to her on the phone, 'and have a drink, but not to read my letter.'

He was right about that.

At other times this kind of routine nastiness can seem scarier, especially if there's intimidation involved. My niece's death threat hasn't been the only one I've received, either by letter or on our website. When the Forced Marriage Unit held a launch for the Forced Marriage Act in November 2008 I was invited to be the keynote speaker at an event in Leicester, but I had to withdraw on police advice after some other Asian guy went on the Karma Nirvana website saying he knew I was going to be there and he was going to 'get me'. The police had already by that stage installed a panic alarm in the Karma Nirvana offices and shown me how to look under my car for bombs.

We've had human faeces smeared on the office windows. I've had to change my mobile number three times.

But now, here, in India, faced with this search for my sister and this total sense of the unknown when I wonder what I'm heading into, I have to admit that I am struck with a fear that I've never experienced before. What am I letting myself in for?

Despite my fantasies of a warm welcome, I have no illusions about Bachanu. From all I've heard, ever since my father first described her to me on the allotment all those years ago, I know she is a poor woman, by Western standards probably an uneducated woman. One of my sisters once said that she and her family still went to the toilet in the fields. My mother always told her daughters to put a lock on their suitcases when they visited her, in case she stole their stuff. I even remember my sister Lucy saying she once had a blazing argument with Bachanu because she had stolen things out of her case and blatantly denied it. But she's my one surviving relative. She's all I have.

There are so many questions I want to ask her.

What do you remember about Dad? What was he like as a young man, before he made the decision to leave and come to the land where the streets were paved with gold? Did he really dance the bhangra *under that tree with earrings in his ears? What did he stand for?*

I'm secretly hoping that Dad was a bit of rebel. That maybe his decision to come to the UK was looked on as brave or unconventional at the time. Perhaps (I think) I am not the only one in the family to have kicked over the traces. Wherever I go I'm always asked the question, 'Jasvinder, why were you different from your sisters? Why were you the one to rebel?' I want to know. Was there someone else in my lineage who was a bit like me? Was it him?

What other family did Dad have over here? And Mum too, what was her family like?

This is something else I know nothing about. Apart from Bachanu's mother, Mum's elder sister, I have no idea about any other family members who might be over here. When I was a child, I wasn't interested; by the time I was old enough to care, I'd left home, so these were questions I never got to ask. I remember Mum once said that Dad had a brother, but she described him as *paagal,* which is Punjabi for crazy. I asked, 'What do you mean, *paagal,* Mum?' She said, 'He's mad. He wanders round the village every day and nobody goes near him.'

Then one time we had a visit in Derby from an old man whom my parents called Bai. He had a long white beard and wore very traditional Sikh dress: a tall white turban on his head, and below that a long skirt with a jersey that went to his knees. Apart from that, all I can remember is that he used to sit in the corner of our living room huddled round the gas fire because he was always so cold. I think he was some sort of grandfather, but whether on my father or mother's side I have no idea.

Do you remember Dad being married to your mother before she died of snakebite? Or were you too small? Did she die of snakebite? How did you feel when my mother married your father?

I'm longing to know about that relationship between Bachanu and my mother. Though my mother visited every year, I suspect that they might not actually have got on that well. After all, my mother replaced Bachanu's mother in my father's life. Perhaps Bachanu resented her. From the photographs I have of Mum over there, on her visits to the village, I get the impression that Mum was something of a peacock when she turned up. She had authority and suitcases full of goodies and everyone flocked to see her. When I look at the pictures of my sisters' weddings she has one hand on the head of the bride, the other on the head of the groom, and this really smug grin on her face, as if she were the centre of everything, which in a sense she was.

Do you remember my sisters coming over and getting married? What was that like in each case?

I want Bachanu to fill in those big gaps for me, those months when Ginda and Yasmin and Robina vanished from Derby, to come back no longer girls, but young women, with their suits and jewellery and strange new subdued and responsible air. Did any of them not want to be married? Did any of them put up a protest while they were here? Lucy confided in me that she had told Bachanu she didn't want to marry the man I had rejected. Does Bachanu remember that? Is it something she would talk frankly to me about?

Does she know how all those marriages worked out?

What have the family told her about what happened to Robina? Or Yasmin's first husband Avtar, who also committed suicide, electrocuting himself, I was told, by putting his fingers in a light socket? Or Prakash's first husband Bila, who drank himself to death? I'd be prepared to bet that whatever she knows, it's an edited version of the truth.

What was it like for you, saying goodbye to your father, not seeing him again for so many, many years?

My understanding from my father was that Bachanu always wanted to come to the UK. Desperately, even. But my father could never get a visa for her, so she never came. Then, when he died, Ginda sent an old-fashioned telegram to Kang Sabhu to inform her of her father's death. Bachanu rang the house in Dale Road and it just so happened that as I was one of my father's executors, I was there, on my own, looking through his stuff, sorting out his affairs. So I took the call. She had no idea who I was, but she was in floods of tears. 'He's my father,' she was saying. 'Please, please, tell them I want to come to England for the funeral.' When I put the phone down I was racking my brains, wondering if there was any way I could make this happen. Then I thought, 'Who am I, of all people, to call her over – most of the time my sisters barely recognise me.' The next day I asked Ginda what we should do. 'Just leave it,' she said. 'She's never been here before. We'll leave it.'

What was it like when Dad reappeared for his last holiday? How did you get on? Was he all you had hoped he would be?

How had my father changed in Bachanu's eyes, from the person she remembered and carried in her head all those years? Did they just slot back together easily – or was it awkward? Did she resent the fact that in some ways he had abandoned her? He had tried to get her over to the UK and failed, but had he told her that? He had never been back. Did she feel rejected? If she did, did she summon up the courage to tell him?

There are so many other details about her life that I want to know too. How old was Bachanu when she got married? Does she have any children – if so, are they married? Where do they live, do they have children too? These are questions, of course, that my sisters would know most of the answers to – but that route is closed to me now. In any case, I want to hear everything from her.

Then, after all that, I want to ask her the most difficult question of all: *What do you know about me?*

What has she been told? When I first called my mother and father after I ran away my mother told me I was dead in their eyes. Was this the official story, exported to Kang Sabhu, to save the family from shame? That I had actually died? Or did the extended family know what I had done? I remember once running into an old school friend, Habiba Ahmed, at a bus stop in Derby. She looked at me as if she'd seen a ghost. 'I thought you'd died years ago,' she said. 'That's what they told us.'

From that central question will flow many others. If Bachanu does know what I did, what does she think of it? Does she have the same attitude as my sisters? Will she reject me out of hand, without wanting to hear my side?

I would love to tell her what it has been like for me, pushed away from my family like this over all these years. I would love to tell her exactly what I do now and why; how my past and my pain has propelled me into this life of campaigning, of trying to change these things that I see as so terribly wrong.

Will she listen? Will she understand? I have no idea. It's a conversation I've never even had with my own sisters. Yes, I've written *Shame*, and it's all documented in the pages there, and they can read that. But I have never once sat down with any of them, face to face, and said, 'Do you know how you made me feel? How I felt when I gave birth to my children and you weren't there? When every birthday passed and I never received so much as a card or a call from any of you? Do you know what it was like walking away from my dead mother alone while you embraced and consoled each other as a family should?

I can't describe the pain of losing your family, of waking up in the morning and knowing you will never see them or be with them again, and then being made to feel it's some-how all your fault. You are somehow the transgressor. When all you did was say, 'I don't want to marry a total stranger.' And then having to live with that rejection and transferred guilt every single day of the rest of your life.

Even when I got back on some kind of terms with my mother and father, at the end of their respective lives, I never asked them those questions, never told them how I felt. I didn't want to risk losing them again and in any case I almost understand why they did what they did. They were just acting within what they knew: Dr Mitra's frozen values. It wasn't a conversation I ever had with those sisters with whom I did rebuild something, either. Even with Robina and Lucy, during those periods when we were back in touch, it always just got left. I didn't want to jeopardise the present, the fact that we were there and together.

If Bachanu and I are to have a relationship, it will have to be with me as I am now, with all that that entails. A lot of water has flowed under the bridge since I left home, and I suspect my family would probably accept me today if I didn't do what I do. But I'm sorry. I am what I am, and I'm not prepared to change. If Bachanu wants to start trying to arrange Jordan's marriage or something, I'll be saying, 'Hang on a minute, I don't *think* so.'

What d'you know about my family now?

Finally, of course, I want to ask Bachanu about her relationship with my family today. What does she know about everyone in England? What has she been told, not just about the successes or failures of my generation, but the next one, the children of these marriages? Does she know about other members of the family who have been disowned? Prakash's second son Ranjit, who would not marry the woman he was supposed to; Yasmin's Bobby, who wouldn't go through with his arranged marriage and ran away? Another of Yasmin's children, a daughter from her second marriage, who ran away from home just like me? Bachanu met Sunny many times, when he came over with my mother, and then, finally, on the trip with my father. But does she know how he is now?

And what of my three children? If she knows I'm still alive, does she know about Natasha, Anna and Jordan? I would love her to be closer to us. When Natasha marries next year, it would be wonderful for Bachanu to come over to the UK and be part of that. It's my dream that she takes on a role at that wedding and brings to life all the things I don't understand. I know Natasha would love that too.

Before Tony and I leave Delhi, we do a little sightseeing. We visit the Red Fort, one of the city's major landmarks, built by a Mughal emperor in the seventeenth century and used by the British as a military camp until they departed at Independence in 1947. It's a massive structure that lives up to its name, with towering terracotta sandstone walls. Being Sunday, the place is packed with visitors, almost all of them Indian. They snake away from the entrance gate in two long queues, one for each gender. The men are in Western dress: long-sleeved shirts, jeans, trainers or sandals; the women are far more colourful, an array of saris of the brightest colours: orange, crimson, electric pink, pale green, dark green, turquoise, yellow; patterned or in two or more colours, many dazzling with swirling floral patterns of silver sequins.

Tony, being six foot five, bulky, white, and with a shaved head, stands out. Once we're inside, standing on the long green lawns between the different buildings that make up the fortress compound, people gather, smiling shyly. Boys run towards him laughing, then dash away again. Young men confer with each other, then approach and ask politely if he will be in a photograph with them. After ten minutes of this, with an ever-increasing crowd around him, Tony receives a marriage proposal. 'Please, sir,' a man asks, gesturing to his daughter, a pretty young woman in a crimson sari, 'will you take her to England, sir, please?' Tony shrugs and smiles, but the man is serious. 'You can take her, sir,' he persists. 'She can be your wife.'

We are both laughing, but there is a genuine intent here. I have little doubt that if Tony handed over his phone number, he could be married to this young lady within days. England has this reputation, as a place where you can prosper and then in due course call others over to prosper too.

This incident is trivial enough, but it makes me aware once again, and all too seriously, of the price British-Asian girls have on their heads, from the moment they are born.

The night before we leave Delhi I lie in bed wondering what lies ahead. The best possible thing that could happen is that I find my sister and she doesn't reject me. She receives me. She shares with me the photos I've brought: old ones of our parents and new ones of my children. We talk about them, we talk about my father's past, we even discover we have things in common; enough that we can be in each other's lives in the future.

The worst thing hardly bears thinking about. She could reject me. And if she does, it will feel as if, after 29 years of hard work rebuilding my life away from the family that has disowned me – I am right back in that place again. If she tells me that I'm dishonourable, that I'm not worthy of human existence, in the same way my family has – I'm not sure I could bear it.

7

6.00 a.m. We are on our way north to Jalandhar, out in the misty dawn with a pile of *mooli paratha* wrapped in silver foil for breakfast. At this time of the morning, the roads are emptier, but the driving is just as crazy. '502 Old Delhi' say the orange lights on a looming bus. A green and yellow motorised *tuk-tuk* shoots past on the inside, faster than it ever would in the day. 'Blow Horn' reads the hand-painted orange letters on the back of a swerving lorry – an unnecessary command, as already the klaxons are blaring.

After one day of observing the Delhi traffic, Tony abandoned the idea that we might hire a car for the long drive north. It will only get worse, David Grahame warned us, once we leave Delhi and the whole mobile dodgem track speeds up on the open road. But this being India, a vehicle with a driver is still relatively inexpensive, and having someone who knows how to manage the challenges of the local traffic seemed to us both to be worth it. As a policeman who has attended many road accidents, Tony is pragmatic about the risks of driving.

So this morning we have taken possession of a four-wheel-drive Toyota Qualis, in a deep maroon. Its big wheels and high chassis mean that we get an excellent view. At the wheel is Inder Singh, our driver. He is a Punjabi Sikh who has come recommended by our friends at the High Commission, a tall, square-shouldered man with a neat moustache and a reserved and respectful manner. When we got to the car he stepped out, opened the back door and showed us in. Out on the road he is skilful and apparently unflappable. From the back seat I watch his thoughtful chestnut eyes flicking between all three of his mirrors as he negotiates the stream of vehicles swirling around him.

The elegant pillars and arches of Connaught Place gleam white in the twilight. We drive on past Delhi's version of Marble Arch, the mighty red sandstone and granite India Gate, built by the British to honour the Indian soldiers who fought for the Raj in the First World War, and are soon away from the green parkland of the centre and bumping through a crowded northern suburb. Muddy puddles and litter line the edge of the road. A crowd queues for *chai* at a street stall. A dog watches a tall bearded man in a white fez and long white robe yabbering away on a mobile phone. We pass the huge bulk of the Red Fort on the left, then we are out on the famous 'GT Road', the Grand Trunk Road, one of South Asia's oldest and longest highways, which runs 1600 miles, from Bangladesh, across northern India, through Pakistan to Kabul in Afghanistan.

Begun by a Maurya emperor in the fourth century BC, rebuilt by the Pashtun conqueror Sher Shah Suri in the fifteenth century, extended by the Mughals, improved by the British, the GT Road has been one of the key trade routes of the region for centuries. A hundred years ago, Kipling wrote, 'Look! Brahmins and chumars, bankers and tinkers, barbers and bunnias, pilgrims and potters – all the world going and coming . . . Truly the Grand Trunk Road is a wonderful spectacle. It runs straight, bearing without crowding India's traffic for fifteen hundred miles – such a river of life as nowhere else exists in the world.' I wonder what the great chronicler of the Raj would make of the mobile traffic jam it is now, three lanes of cars and lorries weaving in and out of each others' way as fast as they can go.

For me, though, its story is personal. I have heard about the GT Road since I was a child. This was the route my mother took to Jalandhar. She never spent time in Delhi, that was just an airport where a relative would pick her up or a car would meet her. Then she would be out here, very likely with one of my sisters beside her.

For my mother this would have been an empowering journey. Back in the UK she didn't speak English, she worked at the local factory, her life was just the little bit of India within the four walls of our house, the trip out to the Asian shops or down to the *gurdwara* at the end of the street. Out here she spoke the language, she wore the clothes, she knew and loved the food, she fitted in. Added to that, she was really somebody. When she came with a daughter, not only was she maintaining the old traditions of arranged marriage, she had credibility and status because she was from England. To all who met her, she sent out the message, 'You are going to prosper from me and my family because I have a daughter from England.'

But what would my sisters have been feeling? Were they frightened? Excited? Did they even know what they were there for? Yasmin did, I know that. But what about Robina, who had been told that she could come out and take a look at her groom, and at India, see how she liked it, before making her final decision? There was no way back for her now, was there, as the realisation slowly dawned that she'd been tricked, that she was coming out to be married after all. There was no Forced Marriage Unit to call in those days. She was in the middle of nowhere, with a woman bent on marrying her to a stranger, and that was that.

Then I think of Lucy, who ended up with the man I was meant to marry. Her sister had run away from home and now she was being taken to the wedding that should have been her sister's. How must that have felt? Prior to that, after I'd run away, my parents had let her have so much more freedom than any of us had ever had. She could cut her hair, dress in Western clothes, go out to pubs and night-clubs. And now, suddenly, she was here – a million miles away from all that.

As I look out of the window, I can't stop thinking about them all, journeying up this same long road with my mother. Thirty years ago, when I should have gone, I doubt it was even two lanes, let alone three. Maybe there would have been potholes to avoid or long traffic jams. Or perhaps it would have all been simpler, fewer mechanised vehicles and more carts and rickshaws and bicycles. But Mum and my sisters would still have been looking out of the car window at the same sights.

There are slums to the left of us now; makeshift shacks stretch from the road's edge right up to tattered terracotta apartment blocks a hundred yards away, the walls above their little balconies stained black with dirt. Schoolboys in white shirts and dark uniforms run for the bus. How do they keep so neat, living in these places? Behind, a huge orange sun rises through the murk; there's a nasty sulphurous smell in the air. On giant mounds of garbage, men and women pick away, looking for anything valuable in the rubbish. What caste are they, I wonder. Are they *chamar*, the caste that Natasha's father Jassey comes from? When I married him, my mother said, 'You've married the lowest of the low, the *chamar*. In India they would be your servants.' I knew that already, because there was a woman who lived down the street from us in Dale Road who used to come and do chores in our house, including massaging my mother's stomach. She was *chamar*, so Mum got her to do menial stuff – that was her role. 'If you ever go to India,' Mum went on, 'you'll see for yourself what they do out there.' She described to me how my caste, the *jatts*, would be on the farm, working the land that they owned, while the *chamar* would be picking up excrement off the streets. 'That is what they do. They pick up poo.'

Now there's a vast encampment of tarpaulin roofs,

stretching for miles. It looks like a refugee camp, but when we ask Inder Singh, it turns out that these are pilgrims coming to hear the preaching of a Sikh guru, Nirankari Sant Samgan, the grey-bearded, white-turbaned old man whose portrait poster is hung on every roadside lamp post. To me, he doesn't look that different to Guru Nanak, the founder of Sikhism, whose picture was in every room in our Derby home when we were growing up.

Dad hardly ever went to the *gurdwara*, but religion was so important to Mum. She went most days of the week, and on Sunday she would take us with her. Before you went in you had to take your shoes off and leave them on a special rack, then cover your head with a scarf or cloth. Once inside, you walked up to the platform at the front of the *gurdwara* and bowed to the man who was slowly turning the pages of the Sikh Holy Book – the Guru Granth Sahib. He wore a big turban and held in his hand a stick that he would waft from left to right. At the end of it was a horse's tail, and every time he turned a page of the Holy Book, he would waft the stick again. While you were up there, you would also put money into a receptacle in front of the platform. After that you'd take your place on the carpet, walking respectfully backwards away from Guru Granth Sahib to get there. Everyone sat on the floor, cross-legged, the men on the right hand side and the women on the left. You couldn't stretch your legs out, that was strictly disallowed. The services could last up to three hours. As kids, it would feel like forever, your legs aching, you yourself unable to move or talk.

Sikhism as I now understand it is a beautiful religion.

But to me growing up, it always seemed to be about restrictions. We weren't allowed to eat beef, we weren't allowed to wear make-up, we weren't allowed to go out with boys, we weren't allowed to cut our hair. When I had my teenage rebellion and had my waist-length mane chopped off at the neck and permed, part of Mum's fury was because this was against the tenets of her religion.

One time I was in the *gurdwara* with my mother and I dared to ask about the caste system. I must have been about nine years old and I was puzzled by it, this ranking of people into groups they could never escape from. I thought, 'I know that she thinks this holy man is important, so I'll use that to try and understand.' I said to her, 'Did Guru Nanak believe in the caste system, Mum?' She didn't reply, so I tried again. 'Look at the people in here, Mum. I know men and women are sitting on separate sides, but we don't have our different castes written on our backs, do we?' At that, she just whacked me across the head so hard. She didn't say anything, but I knew from experience that meant 'Shut up!' It was only when I got much older and studied Sikhism as part of my degree that I understood that one of the founding tenets of the religion was the abolition of the caste system.

Not that Mum was alone in thinking caste had some place in her faith. When I was about twelve, we stopped going to the *gurdwara* at the end of our street and went to one that had just opened across town. It took much longer to get to, and when we got there it was full of a completely different crowd, which was hardly surprising, as this was a *gurdwara* dedicated to *jatts*, our exalted caste. *Chamars* couldn't enter; they had their own place now. Nor was it just in Derby that this bizarre religious apartheid sprang up, unjustified by any of the writings of the Holy Book the worshippers supposedly held as sacred. Other Sikh cities in the UK had – and still have – caste-based *gurdwaras* too. Bradford is full of them. This one for *jatts*, this one for *ramgarhias*, this one for *chamars*.

The straggling monster city that is Delhi gradually gives way to strips of countryside. Here and there are bold housing developments. 'Sharma Properties – to Finance Your Dreams at Divine City'. Finally there are cornfields and trees. This is Haryana Province, where the Government recently upheld the rights of *khap panchayat* (village councils) to adjudicate on the question of inter-caste marriages. Hardly surprising that it is perhaps the worst state in India for honour killings, as is becoming clearer day by day from reading *The Times of India*.

TWO ARRESTED FOR HONOUR KILLING IN HARYANA

FATEHABAD (Haryaba): In a case of honour killing over caste, a young man in Haryana's Jind district was murdered by his wife's brother and an accomplice for belonging to a different caste, police said Sunday.

Sukhbir Singh, in his early 20s and a resident of Rajgarh village in Jind district, was killed by his wife's brother, Jagjit Singh, and his accomplice Friday, police said.

Police arrested both the accused late on Saturday evening.

'Jagjit Singh and his accomplice waylaid Sukhbir near Tohana town (around 20km from here), while he was going to Hisar. They hit his bike with their car and opened fire at him. It is a clear case of honour killing,' said Suresh Kaushik, deputy superintendent of police, Fatehabad, here. 'Sukhbir married Karandeep Kaur of Peepaltha village (in Fatehabad district) in May against the wishes of her family members, who opposed the alliance because of the caste difference,' he said.[2]

Now roadworks start to appear. We slow down to follow big yellow diversion signs, join a single file of traffic trailing round mounds of fresh earth, signs saying 6 Laning and Caution Drive Slow. We slow to pay tax at a roadside checkpoint and suddenly we have crossed into the Punjab. My father's state! This is open country now. The double track road is lined with tall eucalypti, their trunks gleaming white in the mid-morning sunshine. After half an hour we stop for a tea break at a roadside restaurant. The two-storey building is set well back from the road, surrounded by colourful terrace tables and giant plastic toy-like objects: a squatting deer, two white mushrooms, a yellow-beaked swan sitting on top of a log, a bespectacled monkey reading a book, a duck in a grey and white spotted headscarf that doubles as a rubbish bin.

There's some kind of celebration going on on the lower floor of this building. Maybe it's even a wedding. A gaggle of teenaged girls in bright saris run past giggling, then a group of tall men in colourful turbans emerge from a doorway. I'm standing with Tony having a cigarette on the terrace when I find myself reaching over to a nearby ashtray to stub it out.

'Don't you want to finish it?' Tony asks.

I gesture with my head at the Sikhs. 'It's not really the done thing for women to smoke.'

Tony raises his eyebrows. I can see that he's surprised that this campaigner for the rights of Asian women should want to stop smoking in front of a group of strange men, but for me it's ingrained. I was brought up with the idea that women don't smoke or drink, certainly never in front of men or elders. It's wrapped up with all the other things my parents taught me: about morality, humility, respect for others. Some of their values were oppressive, but those things weren't. I guess, when I think about it, that stubbing out my cigarette comes under the category of respect for others. I am in India, so I should abide by local customs. I don't want those guys looking at me and thinking, 'She smokes. That's so disrespectful. What else does she do?'

Even without the cigarette, we are still the subject of curious stares.

'D'you think they can tell you're from England?' Tony asks.

'Of course they can! I'm with a white man for a start.'

'I could be visiting. You could be a local. How do they know?'

I shake my head. 'They can tell. Even before I open my mouth.'

Back on the road, to pass the time, I teach Tony a few words of Punjabi. *Sat sri akal*, God is truth, which is our greeting for hello. *Hanji*, yes. Thank you, *Sukra*.

'And if you're talking to someone you respect you add *ji*. So if you were talking to your older auntie, your *masi*, you would call her *masi-ji*.'

'*Masi-ji*,' Tony repeats.

Now we're on a clear stretch of road, speeding past harvested fields, stripped back to bare earth. When I ask Inder Singh about them, he explains that this was the second crop of the year, barley. They'll be planting wheat now, to be harvested in April. The green fields of leafier plants that we see here and there are turnips.

'Or radishes,' he adds. 'What are the white ones called?'

'Turnips.'

'Turnips then.'

Inder slows the car. There's a nasty accident on the other side of the road. A big white truck lies on its side, with at least one car squashed underneath it.

Tony shakes his head. 'That's a definite fatality,' he says. The endless high-speed game of chicken has gone badly wrong.

Away on the left now I can see dirt tracks running off between the fields. Where do they go, I wonder. To a village, somewhere over the horizon? Is this what Kang Sabhu is going to be like, at the end of a long track like that? The only vision I have of my father's village is of that mighty tree at the centre. A dusty open space perhaps. Houses running away. A *gurdwara* to one side.

In this part of the world, everybody who lives in the same village shares the same surname. My father's surname was Kang, because he lived in Kang Sabhu. The Sangheras, my second husband's family, all live in Belga. The Sandhus, the family that two of my sisters married into, all live in Padoori. I was always intrigued by that as a child. Wow, I would think, a whole village with the same surname. How do you tell people apart?

Now I see groups of men sitting under trees in the shade and I know we are getting close. Because this is what Dad always told me about. Sitting under the tree with his friends in the midday heat and in the cool of evening. I saw a version of it in Derby, as a young girl growing up. Dad would take us to the local park at the weekend. We kids would all be on the swings playing. All of a sudden you would look round and there he would be, down on the grass with seven or eight of his friends, all huddled around cross-legged, talking and smoking.

I almost feel as if my parents are with me on this journey. I've been dreaming about them every night, which I never normally do, apart from at those times in my life when I've been in some way desperate. In 2001, when I was in hospital diagnosed with meningitis, Natasha and my nephew Sunny were at the end of the bed and they told me I must have been hallucinating because I kept saying, 'Move out of the way, you're in the way of Mum and Dad and Robina.'

The other time a parent came to me in a dream was in spring 1997, when Tony Blair had just won the election with a huge landslide. My second husband Rajvinder had recently left me for another woman, and I was living in a bedsit with Natasha and Anna, seven months' pregnant with Jordan. I was in my final year at University and I was really low. I was watching Tony Blair shaking everybody's hand in the crowd, grinning like the Cheshire Cat. The song that was playing was 'Things Can Only Get Better'. I turned the TV off and I was suddenly overwhelmed, in floods of tears. Things weren't getting better for me, were they, they were getting worse and worse. 'Why me?' I was thinking. 'What have I done to deserve this?' I fell asleep and when I woke in the night the bed covers wouldn't move. I was trying to pull them towards me but I couldn't. Then I realised this woman was sitting on the end of my bed. It was my mother, wearing a purple suit. That really scared me, because I knew she'd been dead for five years, and here she was, so real I felt I could reach out and touch her. She put her hand up as if to say, 'It's OK. It's all going to be OK.' The next thing I knew I had sunk back into a deep and peaceful sleep.

Later I told my nephew Sunny about this. His eyes opened wide in amazement. '*Masi*,' he said. 'Bib was buried in a purple suit.' ('Bib' was what we used to call my mother.) I'd had no idea. After Mum died my sisters wouldn't let me go near her body because they said I would contaminate it.

Now my parents are back, both of them. They're not doing anything in particular, they're just chat-chat-chatting on this side and chat-chat-chatting on that side. My father keeps going on about some river or other in the Punjab. The whole thing is giving me a headache.

The fields come to an abrupt end and we pass through a couple of busy towns. Stalls line the main road, weighed down with bunches of bananas, piles of green vegetables and red tomatoes, bright baby clothes, Bollywood DVDs, stacks of shoes. Above the rows of shops, the balconies are crowded with signs. Friends Fast Food; Rags – Italy, UK, Paris; Vikram Medical Hall; English Wine & Beer Shop; Cutilite – Anti Marks and Fairness Cream; Lovely Professional University. The double stream of cars and trucks slows and is joined, from all sides, by mopeds, motorcycles, bicycles, *tuk-tuks*, pedal-powered rickshaws, all weaving in and out of each other, horns blaring. There are brightly turbaned Sikhs everywhere.

This is Ludhiana, Inder tells us. 'The highest number of Mercedes on the GT road.'

As we head out of town some of the houses are huge, their rooftop watertanks adorned with sculptures, bigger versions of those outside the restaurant we stopped at earlier: of birds, aeroplanes, footballs. One has a tall weightlifter holding up a giant dumbbell.

'What's the significance of these sculptures?' I ask Inder Singh. 'On the rooftops.'

He laughs. 'They are just for fun. They are often expatriates. From the UK. Or the US or Canada. I would give my left foot that most of those houses are empty.'

Back out into open country we see a gleaming red KFC, on a bend up ahead. Even though Tony and I have been careful what we eat, sticking in Delhi to vegetarian curries, we're both hungry and neither of us, suddenly, can resist the idea of fast food. Inder parks up, and we note the armed guard outside the glass front doors, not a feature you'd expect back home at a KFC. Inder looks set to stay in the car, but Tony is having none of that. 'Come in and eat with us,' he says.

Inside, the waitresses wear red T-shirts reading I'M A

STUDENT OF LICKANOMICS. Phil Collins plays on the sound system. Tony risks a Chicken Zinger meal, I play safe with a veggie-burger. Both are washed down with cold Coca-Cola. Inder waits for his KFC box on a stool at the far end of our raised table, but Tony calls him over. 'Come on,' he says. 'You can't sit on your own.'

'D'you think the locals think Jasvinder is an English Indian?' Tony asks, as we munch our late lunch.

'Yes,' says Inder.

'How would they know?'

'They can just tell.'

'Of course they can tell,' I say.

'Does Jasvinder have a different accent when she speaks Punjabi?' Tony adds. 'From the locals?'

There is a measured pause. 'I would say so, yes,' Inder Singh replies.

We are interrupted by a wild chant coming from behind the cases of fried and battered chicken. The staff have all vanished from the counter and are doing some sort of motivational training routine, hands punching the air. 'KFC is the best!' they chant, 'KFC is the best!' In Punjabi.

As we leave, the manager stands on the steps, next to the armed guard, and thanks us personally for eating with them. The restaurant has only been open a month, he says.

'It certainly looks like it,' I say. 'Very smart. And your toilets are the cleanest I've seen in India.'

'Thank you, madam,' he says, bowing slightly.

It's certainly not the kind of experience, Tony and I agree, that you'd get at a KFC in the UK.

Forty-five minutes later we pull into an altogether larger town. It's Jalandhar. And here, after fifteen minutes of urban sprawl on either side of the road, is our hotel, the Jalandhar Country Hotel and Suites, right bang on the GT Road, only a small car park separating the front steps from the slowly crawling double snake of traffic heading north.

Inside it's far grander than our cosy little guest house in Delhi. Four storeys of wrought-iron balconies run round a central, marble-floored atrium. In front of the open staircase up to the first floor is a tall wooden arch, within which stands a marble fireplace topped by a long mirror. On this is an elegant glass vase, containing a selection of pampas grasses. Hanging high above is an elaborate chandelier.

Our rooms are equally splendid: a huge double bed on one side, comfy sofas and chairs on the other, a 48-inch-screen TV. I can hardly believe it! We have made it to Jalandhar, the town to which my mother would have brought my sisters to buy their wedding gowns. We are just a stone's throw from Kang Sabhu.

After a quiet dinner with Tony in the restaurant, I retreat to bed and watch an old Bollywood movie. It's *Sholay*, a famous film Mum and Dad used to take us to see as children, in the Asian cinema in Derby. That was always an occasion. All us girls would get dressed up in our finery and drive off to this place called The Spot, which is where the cinema was. Instead of Coke and popcorn, they sold *chai* and samosas. The place would be packed with Asian families. You'd be there for hours, with several intervals. Afterwards we'd play the video on our old VHS machine at home, singing along to all the familiar songs. Films like *Sholay* were old-fashioned and traditional; there was none of the skimpy clothing you get in Bollywood movies today. If somebody was about to kiss, the camera would cut away to a flower. Or the moon or the sun. The values in the films matched those we were brought up with at home. The odd thing is that nowadays, Asian people in the UK watch these racy modern Bollywood films, yet the values they still live by are stuck in the past. Kissing and wearing what the actors wear on screen would lead to many British Asians being shunned in their communities.

I lie in my huge bed, humming along to the songs, enjoying myself as I remember the plot and all the actors. For a couple of hours I'm taken out of myself, wafted straight back to childhood, to the good side of growing up in an Asian family.

Back in Delhi – was it only last night? – I was wondering what Bachanu might know about the next generation of my family, the children of my brother and sisters. Of course she knows something about Robina's Sunny, because he has been out here often. But what of the others: Prakash's three boys: Manjit, Ranjit and Daljit; Ginda's two children, David and Sereena; the five kids that Balbir had with Dawn: Emma, Craig, Ricky, and two others whose names I don't even know; Yasmin's two boys from her first marriage to Avtar: Jimmy and Bobby or the other kids she's had with her second husband; or Lucy's boy, Taran, whose father was a white guy with dreadlocks from Wales?

Some of that generation have had children too, and at this point my knowledge of the family dries up completely. I know Sereena's had a couple of kids, but I've no idea of their names. Manjit and Baljit were married years ago and they have offspring too. But I have been cut off from the rest of them for too long now to know names and details. It's sad how quickly it all seems to have happened. One moment you're not talking to your brother and sisters; the next you've lost touch with an entire generation of your own family, people for whom you are no more than a subject of stories, and probably not very flattering ones at that.

If I do find Bachanu in Kang Sabhu, and she does receive me, it may turn out that she knows more about my lost family than I do. Because even though I was close to some of them when they were little, the rejection of my parents and siblings was, by and large, passed down to their children. I guess it's inevitable that they learned from their parents a similar hot-and-cold, take-her-or-leave-her attitude.

I was very close to Ginda's David when he was a little boy. I changed his nappies so often he started to call me 'Mum' at one point. Other times he woke up at three in the morning crying for me and Ginda had to meet me half way down the street, clutching this screaming bundle in her arms. He would then come back and spent the rest of the night with me at Mum and Dad's. When I ran away the family even used him as bait to try and get me back home to be married, telling me that he was crying his eyes out about me, missing me so much he was ill. That was cruel. I missed him so much myself that I used to get Jassey to drive me the four hours from Newcastle down the motorway to Derby, just so that I could park up outside Dale Primary School and watch him through the fence playing with his friends. It gave me some comfort that they all looked so carefree. At least *he's* not old enough to hate me yet, I used to think.

Much later, when I moved back to Derby after Robina's death and Ginda split with Shinda for a while, and for a few months I was acceptable again, I was reintroduced to David, who was by that stage a teenager. Sadly, he had no memory of the happy times we'd had when he was a child. I was just the *Masi* who had run away, the horrible person who had left him behind. We never recovered the special bond between us.

Around this time I also got to know his younger sister Sereena. Later, when she was at college, she asked me for help with her social work degree. She wanted me to supervise her dissertation. After that, she volunteered at Karma Nirvana for a while and then she joined the staff.

But even though she was working with me, and for me, and I was helping her studies, we never socialised together. I used to hear her talking on the phone to Ginda about parties and weddings they were going to at the weekend, but they never involved me. When I dropped her off at home, it would always be a few doors down the street, so there was no danger of me running into her mother.

Sereena started dating this Sikh guy. Luckily he was right up her street as far as the family were concerned, a well-to-do businessman, and a *jatt* just like us. The family made sure that the relationship soon led to an engagement. To do her credit, Sereena invited me to the wedding.

That brought Ginda back on the phone. 'I can't do anything about Sereena inviting you to the wedding,' she said, 'but I personally don't want you there. If you do come, you'll have to sit at the back.'

Which is what I did. I sat at the back of the *gurdwara* with my children for the whole ceremony. I wanted to be there for my niece and return her compliment in inviting me. I never told Sereena what her mother had said. After she was married, she stopped working at Karma Nirvana and got a job elsewhere. I didn't hear from her after that. She was now a respectably married woman and I suppose I had served my purpose.

As for the others, my relationship with them has

followed a pattern. If they are conforming, doing what they are supposed to do, falling in with the marriage arranged for them, or otherwise being respectable, they have left me alone. If on the other hand they have rebelled, they more often than not have come to me when they needed me.

Yasmin's son Bobby refused to comply with his arranged marriage, so he had to leave home. Later Bobby got in touch with me about another relative who had also refused her marriage. I contacted the police, but unfortunately, rather than going to the girl's school to speak to her direct, they went to see her parents. According to Bobby, within a few weeks she had been taken to India. I hope she knows I am there for her if she needs me.

Following this simple rule, the one member of that generation, and the entire family, that I am still in touch with regularly is my nephew Ranjit, Prakash's second son, known to us all as Gugsy. He fell in love with a woman of a different caste and despite Prakash's attempts to buy him off, he went ahead and married her, after which Prakash disowned him. But even before that he and I always got on well. He was one of the three little boys I helped look after when I was sent off to live with Prakash in London as a young teenager. To this day Gugsy still remembers how I would get between him and Prakash's stick when she was disciplining them. 'Don't hit them,' I would cry, holding up my arm. So I would get whacked instead.

I felt sorry for Ranjit (and his brothers) because their dad Bila died when they were still little. Gugsy must have been around nine. There was no love lost between me and

Bila, but he was still their father, and it was no fun for them to lose him to alcoholism at such a young age. Then, all of a sudden, the boys were being introduced to a new stepfather. Not only was Gurmal the type to try and rule the roost at home, but here was a man who also, quite openly, had another wife in India. I know Gugsy really struggled with that. When he talks about his mother he says she's completely brainwashed to the situation. When Gurmal goes to India every year, he stays with this wife and when she comes to England, she stays at Gurmal and Prakash's house in Slough. Gurmal lets her come there. Prakash moves onto the sofa while they sleep together upstairs.

Sadly, Gugsy's first marriage didn't work out and when I bought my little house in Oakwood in 1997, he came to live with me for a while. My son Jordan was a tiny baby at that time, and it was nice for me to have company, not to mention help with the babysitting. We had a kitchen-diner downstairs with a big wooden table and after I'd got the kids to bed, Ranjit and I would sit up and chat away for ages. I was working hard. I had my day job at Karma Nirvana and I used to work several nights a week as well in this bar called Time, just so I could pay for childcare. I was breast-feeding Jordan, so I used to express milk and leave it in the fridge. One day I came in late from an evening shift at the bar and found Ranjit. He would always wait up for me. As he boiled the kettle to make me a cup of tea, I suddenly remembered I'd forgotten to get milk on my way home. 'Sorry, Gugsy, there's no milk left,' I said, 'and now the shop is shut. I'll have to have it black.'

'Yes, there's milk,' he said, gesturing at his cup. 'I found a little bottle of it in the fridge.'

'Gugsy,' I said. 'That's breast milk!'

He had just taken a mouthful of his tea and he spat it right out on the floor. To this day we still laugh about that.

Other times, then and since, we've gone out for drinks together at the pub. On a couple of occasions we've been to nightclubs. Ranjit is a strong, manly guy, and I always feel completely safe with him, safe as well as valued. He said to me once, during one of our chats, 'If I ever meet a woman that I want to settle down with again, I would like her to be like you.'

When I and the children moved to a new, bigger house in Warwick Avenue after Dad's death, Gugsy came with us. Around this time he met and fell in love with a young woman called Balla. She was a *chamar*, like Jassey, so Prakash and the rest of the family were dead against the match. None of them would go to the wedding, so he asked me to be there to represent his side of the family.

'Ranjit,' I said. 'I'd be honoured to be there, but I don't know about any of the rituals you have to do. Nobody's ever shown me those things.'

'Just come to Balla's house on our wedding day and be there for me,' he said.

So I did. Natasha came with me, because she always got on well with Balla.

Not that Gugsy is a total angel. While he was staying with us at Oakwood, he managed to get himself in trouble with the law. He ended up in a young offenders institution in Leicestershire. I would go and see him regularly, partly because I felt he was another misfit in the family and we misfits should stick together. But my sister Prakash would never go. In the end I rang her and had to pretty much beg her to go and visit him.

'This is your son,' I said. 'You should go and see him.'

'He's no son of mine.'

'You must go. He's going through so much.'

'What's it got to do with you anyway?' she replied. There is only so much you can do, so I told her where he was and how to get a visiting order.

In the end, she did visit him; and guess who was there when she turned up? Me. She just looked at me across the crowded waiting room and didn't come over or say anything. But when the time came to see Ranjit we both had to go in together, because there was only one slot. She was still not speaking to me.

When she got in she sat down opposite him and said 'Hello'. That was that. She didn't say another word.

'Shall I leave?' I asked.

'No,' she said.

So I did the talking and she just sat there. Ranjit was trying to have a conversation with her, he was asking after the family and telling her that his time in prison had made him think about a lot of stuff from his days at home. He was giving her an opening to talk about what had happened between them; I think he even wanted to apologise for some of the times he had behaved badly, especially with regard to her second husband, his step-father, Gurmal.

I was desperately trying to get her involved. I didn't

want to think that Gugsy was going to have the same relationship with his mother that I'd had with mine for all those years, until she finally showed me a chink of light just before she died. But no. Just like our mother, Prakash wasn't playing. She sat there silent, like a ghost. When the session was over she left without a word. She didn't say goodbye to me and once again we went our separate ways.

8

In the morning I wake with a spring in my step. When *Sholay* was finished last night I took a couple of sleeping tablets and slept straight through without any troubling dreams of my parents or anything else. Another reason to feel cheerful is that Anup has arrived in India. He flew direct to Amritsar, which is two or three hours north of here on the GT road. I feel a great sense of reassurance now that I know he's here. He may not yet be married to Natasha, but he's still family to me; and I feel as if I need family with me on this last leg of my journey.

Normally when a girl from the UK visits her rural village she makes the journey with her mother and other relatives. I too would have been with my mother if I'd come here to get married. Now I am doing what in many ways is unthinkable. I'm coming on my own, as a disowned woman. So just having Anup at my side is going to make such a lot of difference. I'm not denigrating Tony. He is my good friend and I truly appreciate his support. But he's not family.

Kang Sabhu is only a few miles outside Jalandhar. But we are not going to attempt to make our visit today. We are going to wait till Anup joins us. In the meantime, we'll have a chance to look around Jalandhar, buy a map, work out exactly where Kang Sabhu is.

After breakfast in the hotel, Inder drives us up the busy GT Road for a few hundred yards, then turns left into the centre of town. There's a provincial feel to the place. There are fewer *tuk-tuks* than in Delhi and they're taller, an elegant blue and yellow. The pedal rickshaws have hoods, which are painted in elaborate colours and patterns. As we walk around the central streets, a beggar woman with a baby in her arms follows us. When we give her a few rupees, she is replaced by an old gentleman in a bright orange turban and matching *salwar kameez*. He bows from the waist as he holds out a shiny metal saucepan as a begging bowl.

The banners and signs festooning one little alley we walk down tell their own story. 'Canada visa in just 14 days' says one strung from side to side. Below it a tall board offers 'Embassy interviews, English speaking, personality development'. Learn English, go West, prosper, is the clear message.

I see a shop selling wedding gowns and stop in my tracks. Perhaps this is the very place my mother would have brought my sisters. 'Choose your wedding gown,' she would have said. How often that phrase is repeated by the victims who come to us at Karma Nirvana. 'I went to India, Jasvinder, thinking I was going for a holiday. We got to the town near our village and my mother took me to a shop and said, "Choose your wedding gown, you're getting married." That was the first I knew of it.'

I have heard this story so many times and it makes me so angry. Why don't the families tell the girls back in the UK why they're taking them to India? Of course, really, I understand why. If they did, most of them – Westernised, educated, children of the UK – would do anything they could not to go. But how can these families ever feel that it's acceptable: that there is this deceit around such an important occasion, which will alter and define the rest of their daughters' lives? At another level, why doesn't the Government do something about it? These young women are British subjects. In Bradford alone in one recent summer there were 205 girls unaccounted for; 172 were eventually traced, leaving 33 permanently missing. Multiply that figure across the Asian communities of the UK and you've got hundreds. If these were white girls vanishing from school rolls every year the media would be jumping up and down about it; there would be an outcry.

Here in India shocking things are happening all the time. Every day I look in the papers and see another tragic story. An honour killing here, a burning there. The big difference between here and home, as I've said before, is that here it is overt. The abuse is in the newspapers, it's in your face; at home we have a harder job on our hands, because so much of it is hidden. Of course the really big stories make the news. When there's a murder, and it's proved to be an honour killing, that is a story. But that's once in a blue moon compared to the abuse and coercion that's going on all the time under the radar, ignored or misunderstood by the agencies that should be helping.

Think of poor, bright-eyed Banaz Mahmod, in love for

the first time at nineteen. She had escaped the Kurdish husband who knocked out one of her teeth because she called him by his first name in public. She had met another Kurd whom she genuinely loved, calling him 'my prince' in the numerous text messages found on her phone after her death. The Independent Police Inquiry has just finished reporting on the mistakes made in that case. Before she was murdered, Banaz went to the police *on four separate occasions*, but they didn't believe what she was telling them. Even when she managed to escape from her father, who had forced her to drink half a bottle of brandy and tried to strangle her, and she ran to a nearby cafe, covered in blood, screaming 'They're trying to kill me,' officers attending the scene refused to accept her story. PC Angela Cornes sized up the frightened girl and decided she was 'an attention-seeking drunk.' A month later Banaz was dead, strangled with a bootlace; to 'show her disrespect' her two murderers raped her first.

Fortunately for me, I am not standing in this street being asked by my mother which wedding gown I wish to wear. I send prayers of thanks up to God that my instincts saved me from ever being put in that position. I look round this street of Jalandhar shops – My Foot Shoes; Chahal's Charm; Top in Town, the Family Restaurant – and I think, 'Who could I possibly have asked for help? Where would I have run to? How in a million years could I have got back down the GT Road to Delhi from here?'

I am about to buy a map of the city and surrounding area when Tony has a better idea. We have a day to kill before Anup is here and we're ready to go. Why don't we call in at the relevant Jalandhar authority and not only see a map, but find out a little bit more about Kang Sabhu. Trust an ex-policeman to want to do the job properly. But he's right. It's definitely wise to know as much as we can about the village before we attempt to visit it.

With that in mind we head across town to the Jalandhar Public Records Office. There are two tall policemen in khaki uniforms and crimson turbans guarding the wrought-iron gate outside, but inside it's not an impressive building. The main stairwell smells of urine. A broken sign on the lift reads GENRAL. Upstairs on the first floor we are ushered into an office ahead of a small, seated queue. A white man and a UK-born Asian woman seem to be of sufficient novelty or importance to take precedence. But we soon discover we are in the wrong place. We need the Jalandhar Development Office, we are told. It is there that they will have all the details of Kang Sabhu.

An hour later we have finally located this office, in a nondescript building on a dingy backstreet. Red and blue graffiti adorn its unpainted concrete exterior, and above that its walls are festooned with a dense tangle of telephone and electric wires. Inside, a small, warehouse-like space with opaque glass windows in little rectangles is divided into offices by orange-painted wooden screens. Two bicycles and a moped stand in a central area next to a redundant water cooler; next to that a keg on a table drips water into a bucket. We are shown in to one of the offices, where a young man in a stripy jumper sits next to a colleague in a bright yellow shirt behind a long desk. I explain that I'm from the UK, that I'm looking for a half-sister who I believe lives in the village of Kang Sabhu. My father was born there, his surname was Kang. She is the daughter of his first marriage, who stayed behind when he emigrated to the UK in the 1950s. This perks the guys up no end, and we are soon joined by three or four others: two older, bearded men in turbans, a skinny fellow in a sleeveless jersey, and a sleek-looking gentleman in grey suit trousers and a striped shirt.

Kang Sabhu is indeed within the District of Jalandhar, they tell us, fourteen kilometres from the centre of town, out on the Nakodar Road. They point to a map on the wall. There it is, a little criss cross of streets next to the main road, right out in the Agricultural area, well beyond the Old Built Up City (High Density), the Residential Area (Medium Density) and the Residential Area (Low Density). My heart turns over to see it. I'm ten miles away. How long would that take to drive? Fifteen minutes?

Of course I will find my sister if I go there, these helpful officials tell me. 'It's 100 per cent guaranteed that there will be people in that village who know who your sister is,' says the kindly-looking old gent in the grey turban. 'There will be people in the village who will remember your father and know who he was. You go there,' he says with a smile, 'you'll find them. And they'll be glad to see you.'

I look over at Tony and his face gives nothing away. But he knows what I'm thinking. I've little doubt I'll find people who knew my father; who maybe can take me straight to my sister. But will they be glad to see me? The shamed woman, disowned by her family in the UK, who has been mad enough to break all the rules and travel out here on her own?

The man in the grey turban now tells me that if my father went over to England in the 1950s on a ship, he would have gone from Bombay. The sea journey on to Europe would have taken fifteen days. Now that I have made the journey from Delhi up here myself, that gives me real pause for thought. To travel all the way to Bombay, which is four times as far from here as Delhi, then on into the unknown, to Europe, to make a better life for his children: that speaks volumes about the determination and courage Dad must have had – an almost warrior-like spirit. I feel uplifted. Perhaps I, too, have some of that spirit; perhaps that is why I am here.

If I would like to know more about Kang Sabhu, says the man in the striped shirt, he could look up the census for me; give me an idea of the population, what age it is, how it breaks down in terms of occupation. Of course I'd be interested, I say.

So he leads us upstairs to an altogether smarter office on the first floor. This contains a huge glass-topped mahogany desk, surrounded by black leather and chrome chairs, stacked with piles of papers and yellow ring-bound books. One is stamped MASTER PLAN JALANDHAR. The walls are covered in large-scale maps of Jalandhar.

We introduce ourselves properly. We are from the north of England, we explain: Derby and Cleveland. He is Mr Harbir Singh, he tells us, from Jalandhar. He leaves the office for a couple of minutes and returns with two census books for Kang Sabhu: 1991 and 2001, the most recent. We stand together around the big desk. Tony gestures politely to the only chair with arms. Mr Singh smiles and shakes his head. It's his boss's chair, he says. So we all sit on three armless chairs on the other side of the desk.

Mr Singh leafs through the census book. Here are the facts about my father's village. In 1991 Kang Sabhu had 2259 inhabitants.

'A big village,' he says approvingly.

By 2001, that figure had increased to 2617. So it's a growing village, too.

1385 were male, 1232 were female. There were sixty-nine families. 1560 of the inhabitants were literate.

'Literacy is very high,' says Mr Singh.

Now he looks down the list and starts talking about occupations. 350 were involved in agriculture, 684 in non-agriculture. Looking over at his book, I notice that there are caste distinctions listed as well.

'So were people still registered by caste in 2001?' I ask.

'Yes. Everyone is registered by caste.'

I am, frankly, astonished. After all the talk we've had about how India has moved on, left the caste system behind, here in one presumably typical rural village in the Punjab the official census is still registering the inhabitants by caste. What are the implications of this, I wonder. If people are listed by caste, then there is an almost official sanctioning of the tradition that they marry within caste as well. That would explain a lot about my parents' strict attitude to the matches they arranged for us.

Mr Singh seems unapologetic, if a little embarrassed. 'It

is your profession,' he says with a shrug, and it is clear that he is referring to caste. 'It is what you do.'

I nod. Mr Singh has gone out of his way to be helpful to this pair of random strangers who have turned up on a Tuesday morning in his office. I certainly don't want to alienate him. But I dread to think what he would say if he knew I was a *jatt* who had run away to marry a *chamar*.

'I thought Sikhs didn't have castes?' says Tony. Bless him, he has asked the most leading of leading questions; but being a white outsider from the UK, he will get away with it.

'Not exactly,' says Mr Singh.

'So what are the different castes?'

Mr Singh is happier about answering that. He goes off into a long explanation of how caste was originally a Hindu idea. There were five main groups: the Brahmin, priests; the Kshatriyas, warriors and rulers; the Vaishyas, traders, merchants and officials; the Sudra, unskilled workers; and then at the bottom, the outcasts, known these days as Dalits.

'The untouchables?' says Tony.

Mr Singh shrugs. This is a contentious issue in modern India and it is clear he is not going to get into it.

'So how does that relate to the Punjabi castes?' Tony asks. '*Jatts* and *chamars* and so on?'

'They are similar. But not the same,' says Mr Singh.

'I'll explain later,' I say. Mr Singh looks relieved. 'That is all very interesting,' I add. 'Now perhaps before we go we could have another look at the map.'

As we leave his office Mr Singh is all smiles. He has no

doubt, he reiterates, that when we get to Kang Sabhu we will find my sister. I thank him warmly for his help. There is no way I can tell him what I am really thinking: that in a village in which caste is still not just an unofficial designation but an official one, maybe things won't be so straightforward tomorrow, after all.

Downstairs, the old man with the grey turban is waiting for us. He smiles and nods his head as he follows us out onto the street. He puts his hands together in the *namaste* gesture. I reciprocate. He comes closer. '*Putt*,' he says, 'don't worry, your sister will be there in the village. You will find her.'

That single word *putt* cuts straight to my heart. It is the word my father used to call me when I was a child. I haven't heard it from anyone since he died. I look up at the old man gratefully. It feels almost as if it were my father talking to me.

'Wow,' I say to Tony as we walk on down the street towards the car. 'That was quite something. I'm glad we went.'

'What about the different castes?'

'I had no idea they still documented them like that.'

'I didn't ask the wrong question?'

'You put him on the spot. And you were right. One of the founding principles of the Sikh religion was to get rid of caste.'

'When was the Sikh religion founded?' asks Tony.

'In the fifteenth century.'

'They're taking their time, then.'

I laugh. 'They certainly are.'

At that moment, my mobile rings. It is Anup. He has arrived in Jalandhar and is now at his uncle's house, catching up with relatives. He will be with us at the hotel in the early evening.

'Perhaps we should drive out and have a look at Kang Sabhu,' I say. 'Not stop, but just have a look. Almost like a recce for tomorrow.'

Tony doesn't think that would be a good idea. In a little place like Kang Sabhu there will be people watching every car that comes in and out. 'You don't want people gossiping about you before you've even got there. You don't want to throw away that element of surprise. Imagine if somebody recognised you somehow and phoned your sisters in the UK.'

He's right. I must put my curiosity on hold for another day.

'There's nothing to stop us getting out of Jalandhar for the afternoon, though. Why don't we drive into the countryside in the opposite direction, have a look at that, get a feel for the kind of rural area we'll be looking at.'

'OK, fine, let's do that.'

So Inder Singh consults his map, turns the car round and heads back into the busy centre of Jalandhar. Now that we've agreed that we're not going into Kang Sabhu till tomorrow, I'm happy. I feel as if the date is set. Anup will be with us. There's nothing more I can do now.

'When I get back I'm going to say to the children, "You come from an intelligent village. Use it."'

Tony smiles. 'You do that.'

Outside the window, horns blare. We are marooned on a

crowded roundabout. Right beside us, two women and a small boy are making slightly faster progress than us in a rickshaw with a colourful hood. Even though the hood is folded, you can see, under gleaming brass studs, the bright strips of orange and yellow that make up the canopy. The women are in saris: one a carnation pink, with silvery sequin-work in a floral pattern; the other turquoise and orange. The boy sits up on the lap of the second woman in a brown jersey, blue denims and smart white trainers, picking his nose. The women are chatting and laughing, while the rickshaw man, strong and handsome with a thick, dark, handlebar moustache, pedals doughtily on, weaving skilfully between the shifting lines of traffic. What caste are each of them, I wonder. Will the sons of the rickshaw man still be pedalling rickshaws in twenty years' time?

A little further on, we slow to a halt again, this time for a black cow, which is heading across three lanes of traffic right by a set of lights. Of course I know that the cow is sacred in India, they are allowed to roam wherever they like; but seeing one here, lumbering slowly between the cars and buses and the orange and blue signs for Aircel mobile phones, apparently on its way into the Indian Oil garage, is so incongruous it's comic.

The Kerala Ayurveda Centre; Bobby Chiken Corner (Government Approved Drinking Place); Georgeous; Groovy. The G Series Has Arrived. The endless line of shops and stalls and signs starts to thin on the road out of town. Suddenly there are trees and fields on both sides. Some are recently harvested, with stripped brown stalks flat on the ground; some are newly planted, with fresh green shoots poking through the bare brown earth; some are waist-high with yellow flowers.

'Those are mustard fields, isn't that right?'

'Mustard fields, yes,' says Inder Singh.

A memory flashes back to me, of my mother in England, looking out of the car window at the yellow fields of flowers we saw from the M1 when we were driving down to London to see my sister Prakash in Forest Gate. As soon as Mum saw one she would get all excited and sit up. 'In India, this is what it's like,' she'd tell us. 'Mustard fields like this.' Mustard is central to Punjabi culture and a staple of the traditional cuisine: its seeds are used to make mustard oil for cooking; then in winter, mustard leaves are used in a curry called *Sarson-ka-saag*.

I always knew the English fields weren't mustard, but for a long time I thought they were spinach. One day my daughter Natasha corrected me. She said, 'Mum, you've been telling me since I was five that these fields are spinach, but they're not, they're rape.'

'Rape?'

'Yes. That's what it's called. They make rape seed oil with it.'

'Why on earth didn't you tell me?'

She said, 'Mum, I didn't want to hurt your feelings.'

Typical Natasha, always thinking of others.

Just up ahead there's a little road off to the left under the trees. 'Shall we go up here?' I suggest. Inder slows the car and we bump down and follow it round, past a few farm outbuildings and then out into fields away from the main road. Spreading green trees are dotted here and there, dwindling away towards the horizon. They don't look that different from the trees of home. Apart from the odd oblong field of sugar cane we could be driving across a flat part of Lincolnshire or East Anglia in high summer. Another little mustard field appears and I ask Inder Singh to stop for a moment. He pulls in and we get out of the car.

The only noise out here is the cooing of wood pigeons. To our right, two buffaloes lie in the shade of a clump of eucalyptus trees, quietly munching away at the green grass. There's a pile of hay beyond, under another big shady tree. We're not even in Kang Sabhu yet, but I feel both reassured and excited: this landscape is exactly as my father described it to me. This tree could even be the tree he sat under chatting with his friends.

'I'm just going to take a little walk,' I say to Tony.

'Take your time.'

I leave him by the car and stroll out along the edge of the mustard field. The flowers are slightly smaller than in the rape fields of home, but the effect is the same: a shimmer of yellow bobbing heads, receding into the distance. This was what my father was thinking about, as he let the damp Derby soil fall through his fingers, as on cold March days he planted up his turnips and his onions and his potatoes and his radishes. This is what he gave up to give us, his children, a better chance. Whatever anger I still feel about the way I was treated for all those years, I mustn't forget this. Dad was a brave man and he did a brave and adventurous thing.

At the far end of the long field I come across two women with big, loose bales of hay balanced on their heads. They are simply dressed: one in an orange dress over baggy green trousers; the other a floral pattern over dark brown. Under the bales both their heads are covered with long scarves. On their feet they wear grey plastic sandals.

'*Sat sri akal*,' I say.

'*Sat sri akal*,' they reply, breaking into grins; they have lovely white teeth in dark suntanned faces. Naturally, being Punjabi, they want to know who I am, where I'm from.

I tell them and they laugh.

'England. We've never been to England.' They've heard of it, though, a wet country full of white people, not that they've ever seen one.

'There's one over there,' I say, gesturing to Tony at the far end of the field. They peer over to look at him, shaven headed and six foot five, towering above Inder Singh, smoking a cigarette as they chat together.

'*Hai rabba!*' they say, laughing some more. *Oh my word!* 'Is that what they're like over in England?'

'Some of them,' I say.

'Do you have children?' they ask, quick as a flash.

'Not with him,' I reply and we laugh some more. I tell them I've two girls and a boy. They nod approvingly. The woman in orange has two boys and a girl; the one in the floral patterned dress has three girls and a boy.

'I'm one of seven sisters,' I tell them.

'*Hai rabba!* Seven sisters.'

'And they all came out here to the Punjab to get married. When they were sixteen.'

'*Acha.*' *Is that right?*

I look into their warm, friendly faces and decide I have nothing to lose; we are in the middle of a field, miles away from Kang Sabhu.

'I didn't,' I tell them, 'come out here to get married. I told my mother and father I didn't want to get married.'

They both look at me seriously for a moment. 'So . . . did you want to study?' asks the woman in orange.

'Yes, I did. That's it. I wanted to study.'

'*Acha,*' they go, nodding.

'Would you like us to be your *vichollah*?' says the woman in orange and now it's my turn to laugh. A *vichollah* is a go-between, somebody who arranges marriages.

'I'm fine,' I say.

'We can do that for you. Come on! We can find you someone from the village.'

'No, no, really, I'm fine as I am.'

'Get married!' she says. 'It's good to be married. We'll find you somebody.'

'It's fine,' I say. 'I'll pass on that.'

We're all three laughing together now; none of us think for one moment that they mean it.

When I get back to the road, Tony has got chatting to a white-bearded old gentleman with a grey-green *salwar kameez* and a fine sky-blue turban. He stands by a matching sky-blue moped.

'*Sat sri akal*,' I say.

He grins and nods. '*Sat sri akal*.'

'Mr Singh here speaks English,' says Tony.

Mr Singh nods proudly.

'He was just telling me there's a temple down the road,' says Tony. 'In his village. He's offered to show it to us if we'd like.'

Why ever not? It is still early afternoon. We have time to kill. And it would be interesting to get the feel of a typical Punjabi village before we go into Kang Sabhu tomorrow. The old man gets back on his moped and leads us on down the little winding road across the empty fields. A long straight railway line comes into view. His village straddles both sides of a dusty little level crossing, one of those ones with the orange and white barriers that go up and down. Just on the far side he pulls up. There is an arch and beyond it steps going up a little mound.

I had imagined Mr Singh would be taking us to a Sikh *gurdwara*. But at the top of the steps is a Hindu temple. Above the entrance is a little bell, something we Sikhs don't have. Outside stands a terracotta elephant with a sequinned orange scarf around its neck. A young woman with a baby on her hip is sweeping the bare ground with an old-fashioned broom of twigs tied round a central stick. This voluntary work is called *seva*; it means doing a service unselfishly for others, without any thought of reciprocation, and it's a key element of both Hinduism and Sikhism.

Seva was a word used a lot in our house as we grew up. We used to do *seva* in the *gurdwara* in Derby, encouraged of course by my mother. We helped in the communal kitchen or served food to the congregation after the service. For us kids it was a way of earning brownie points with Mum – and her friends. 'Look how good the daughters are,' people would say, 'they are doing *seva*.' We did *seva* at home too, when visitors came round – we would hand round the tray of tea and biscuits with polite smiles. If you were getting married you did even more *seva*, because you were supposed to show visitors what a dutiful daughter-in-law you were about to become.

Here though the *seva* seems pure, unforced, as it's supposed to be. The young woman pauses in her sweeping for a moment and smiles shyly.

We bow our heads to go inside. It's like a Hindu temple in a Bollywood movie. Instead of the Holy Book and the simple carpet of a *gurdwara*, the place is filled with colourful statues and pictures of Hindu gods and goddesses: Sita and Hanuma and Vishnu and the elephant Ganesha. Krishna is right at the centre. Incense sticks are burning and there are garlands of orange flowers hung everywhere.

'So you don't have a *gurdwara* in this village?' I say to Mr Singh.

'No.'

'But you are Sikh?'

'Yes. But Sikhs can worship in a Hindu temple, just as Hindus are welcome in a *gurdwara*. And Moslems, and Christians. Sikhs believe that God is one. And everywhere,' he adds. 'I say my prayers in here.'

We step outside into the dappled shade of the trees that surround the little temple. 'So where are you from?' he asks. 'What are you both doing here?'

I explain that we're trying to find my sister, who lives, we think, not far away, in a village on the other side of Jalandhar.

'Which village is that?'

'Kang Sabhu.'

'Ah, Kang Sabhu.' Mr Singh knows of it, but he doesn't know it. I'm a little relieved at that. I don't go into any more detail, and I don't share my full story with him. He seems like the kindest and humblest of men, but I'm not ready to risk any kind of scene or rejection today. Instead I ask him about my father, as he seems old enough to be of an age with him, certainly to remember those days.

'I know he went to England to make a better life for us, but d'you know why he would have gone? Would he have been invited by the British Government, or would he have made his own way?'

Mr Singh explains that after the Second World War, Sikhs who had fought for the British were allowed to settle in the UK. There were quite a few Sikhs who fought in the war.

'Yes,' says Tony. Only a couple of months back, he says, he saw the obituary of a famous Sikh pilot in *The Times*. (Later, back in the hotel, we look him up on Google: he was Squadron leader Mohinder Singh Pujji, DFC, who died in Gravesend, Kent in September 2010. He flew in the war with the RAF alongside twenty-three other Indian pilots spread among Fighter, Coastal and Bomber Command. He wore a turban in his cockpit, with his wings sewn onto it, specially adapted so his earphones could go over it.)

Then, after the war, Mr Singh goes on, the British Government were looking for unskilled labourers, to make up a shortage in the British work force. 'You could apply to go. Your father would have seen it as an opportunity. He would have had to get a work permit from Delhi, so he would have gone down to Delhi on the bus or the train. With the work permit they would have issued him with a passport.'

'A British passport?'

'Yes.' He smiles. 'They were easier to come by in those days.'

'Then I know that he went from Bombay on the ship.'

'Yes. He would have taken the ship because it would have been much cheaper than the plane. He probably would have paid about three hundred rupees to take the ship, and he would have gone at first on his own, leaving your mother here.'

'He did leave my mother here. For five years. Then he came back to get her.'

'That is what they did,' he says. 'And then she went. And then you became British.'

I smile. With many complications I'm not going to share with you right now, I think.

'Can you tell me one other thing,' I ask. 'My father always wrote and read in Urdu, and he spoke it too. That's something that has always puzzled me.'

'That was normal then. Before Partition, in 1947, Muslim, Sikh and Hindu people lived together, right across the Punjab. Even I remember that. We had many Muslims here. There's a Muslim shrine at the other end of the village that people still visit. All our teaching in school was in Urdu. That's why your father wrote and spoke Urdu.'

When Mr Singh asks what we do in England, Tony tells him he's a retired policeman. Our new friend laughs. He was a policeman too, he says.

At the bottom of the steps we thank him for showing us the temple. 'Not at all,' he says, in Punjabi. 'A guest is like a gift from God. Now perhaps you would do me the honour of visiting me in my house.'

I look over at Tony. He shrugs. 'Whatever you want to do. I expect Anup will be at the hotel by now.'

I look at my watch. It is four o'clock. The shadows are starting to lengthen in the fields.

'I think we should get back to Jalandhar,' I say. I smile apologetically. 'My son-in-law is coming to join us.'

'Ah well.' Mr Singh shrugs and smiles. 'Maybe another time.'

'Perhaps I could take a photograph of you and Jasvinder together,' says Tony.

'Only if she ties a *rakhri* on me,' says Mr Singh.

I smile. A *rakhri*, I explain to Tony, is the symbol of a

brother and sister. Mr Singh takes the hanging scarf part of my *salwar kameez*, the *chunni*, and wraps it tightly round his wrist. 'Now I am your brother,' he says. 'A brother's job is to protect his sister for life. From anything. So if you need protection you can come to me.'

We perform this little ceremony on the dusty concrete road in front of the gate by the steps up to the temple. A little crowd has gathered. Four or five grinning boys, in identical grey sandals, two carrying shiny steel cans that look like mini milk-churns.

There is also a middle-aged man in a blue tracksuit, who seems as if he might be drunk. He has barged in on our conversation unwanted and introduced himself as Johnny. Where are we from, he asks. The UK, fine. Why are we here? He is staying in the village, he tells us, visiting his elderly mother, who is sick. But he actually lives in New York. Manhattan. He has a restaurant there. And a gas station in Delaware. He has lived in the US for thirty years. The only reason he is here is to see his mother. He lives in one of the biggest houses in the village. Actually one of the biggest houses in the Punjab. It cost him $50,000 to build and is worth $100,000 now. Perhaps we would like to go with him and see it.

It is time to go. Sadly this character has spoilt what has been until now an enchanting afternoon. We say a hurried goodbye to Mr Singh and get into the car and drive off.

'What an arsehole,' says Tony.

'It was so annoying how he muscled in like that. He was really showing off.'

'Was any of it even true?'

'He's just one of those Asian peacocks, you know. Who go abroad, earn money, then come back and show off. I hate to say it, but he reminds me a bit of Sunny.'

My very first memory of my nephew Sunny is as a tiny little boy. When Natasha was born, Robina came to see me in hospital and I remember Sunny being fascinated by the new baby, sitting on Robina's knee, holding the edge of the bassinet and blowing kisses to her. Shortly after that, when Lucy left her husband and came to live with me in Bradford, I didn't see Robina for a while. When she got back in touch, she was living in Leicester with Baldev and Sunny was a naughty little boy of six. When I went to visit her he and Natasha played together as little children do.

After Robina died, Baldev had no interest in taking on Sunny, so he was effectively orphaned. Mum and Dad took him in and from then on devoted themselves to bringing him up. But there were certain things they couldn't do, like going into school for parents' evenings or talking to teachers and such like. With their smattering of English, that wasn't really an option. So gradually I got into the way of helping out with Sunny. Then when Mum died, a year and a half after Robina, Dad had Sunny all to himself. It wasn't easy for him. He was in his late sixties, retired, and he was trying to be mother, father and both grandparents at the same time. I would visit them from time to time at our house in Dale Road, but it was never easy, because Dad still couldn't quite admit that he was allowing me back into the family. I always had to phone before going, in case one of my sisters or my brother might catch me there. Not that this stopped Dad calling me if Sunny was in trouble at school.

'He's having problems,' he would tell me. 'They say he's always fighting. Can you go down there and talk to his teachers?'

Sunny was getting older. Kids can be cruel. They would tease him about Robina's death, 'Your Mum set herself on fire, didn't she?' It was hardly surprising he got into fights.

It was tough in many ways for Dad, bringing up Sunny, but he doted on him. Certainly he was more involved with his upbringing than he'd ever been with ours. I remember catching him one afternoon play-wrestling with Sunny on the living room floor. I was amazed; I'd never seen Dad do anything so undignified in my life. 'You can't let the young ones win all the time,' he said, grinning to cover his embarrassment as he sank back, breathless, into his usual armchair.

And of course Dad took Sunny to Kang Sabhu. That was the time I asked him if I could go too, and got the answer that made me feel as if I'd been hit by a stun gun: 'Shame travels, Jasvinder.'

When Sunny was fifteen, Dad died. Sunny was the one who found him. He came back from playing football in the park with his mates to discover him lying on the living room floor, his mouth wide open, his skin pallid and grey. Sunny was crouched beside him when I arrived at the house, tears streaming down his face. Together, we tried to resuscitate him with the kiss of life, but he was beyond our help. When his will was read, Dad had left everything to Sunny: the house in Dale Road and all his savings. My sister Ginda was so furious she walked out of the solicitor's office in disgust. In that same will there was a request that Sunny live with me, which was as much a shock to me as anyone else in the family.

Sunny couldn't stay in Dale Road on his own, so after a short spell with Ginda while I relocated to central Derby, he came to live at ours. I sold the house I'd had in Oakwood, a leafy suburb four miles north-west of the main Asian area, and bought a place on Warwick Avenue, a pleasant street of detached houses on the way to Dad's allotment. When I was a child I had always joked with Dad as we drove down it on Saturday mornings that one day I would live in Warwick Avenue. Now, paradoxically, after he was dead and gone, I finally did. But I did it for Sunny, so he could live with us and be near his school.

Natasha, Anna and Jordan were all living with me too, so Sunny joined the family. But I soon began to notice a change in him, as he started to challenge the way I was and what I stood for. He was a teenager in mid-adolescence, so some of his attitude was understandable, but some of it puzzled and alarmed me. Where did all this stuff come from, I wondered.

'Why can't you be more like Gindi *masi*?' he'd say.

'What d'you mean?'

'She's a respectable Asian woman, married with children. She wouldn't allow her daughter to date. I can't believe you're allowing Natasha to date.'

This was absurd. Natasha was about fifteen at this time and had recently got herself 'a boyfriend', a nice lad of her age who was half white, half Asian. It was hardly very serious. But Sunny was so aggrieved by this relationship that he was saying ridiculous things like, 'I'm going to arrange to have him beaten up and his legs chopped off.'

One time this kid came to the house. He and Natasha were chatting in the front room and Sunny came in, flexing his muscles, screaming and shouting at me, 'How can you allow her to see somebody like this? You've got no respect. Once he leaves the house I'm going to sort him out.'

I told Sunny to stop being silly, but the boy was petrified. When he had gone I had another word with my nephew. 'You can't behave like that,' I said. 'You terrified the poor lad.'

'What do you know?' he snarled at me. 'You're not a respectable Asian woman. You're divorced. You've been divorced twice. Me and my mates, we're going to get him. Teach him a lesson.'

He slammed the door and left. After five minutes I decided I'd better follow him. I had a sudden horrid feeling that he might do what he said. Sunny's Asian friends were like that. They all had the same strict, old-fashioned and dreadfully hypocritical views. Hypocritical because of course if they wanted to fool around with white girls themselves, that was fine. White girls were 'easy meat'. They would have their fun with them and then when the time came to get married, find a nice unspoilt Asian girl. Either from the UK or, more likely, from India. 'When I get married,' Sunny would say, 'I will never marry a woman like you. And I'd never want my wife to meet you either.'

I ran after Sunny and caught up with him just as he and his friends were about to batter this poor lad. They were all standing round him in a back alleyway.

'If you lay one finger on him I'll call the police,' I yelled at them.

They backed off and let him go; that was the last we saw of him. Natasha was understandably furious. After that incident Sunny moved out and went to live with Ginda for a while. 'I am going to live with the decent *masi*,' he told me.

But that didn't last long. He soon came back. The decent *masi* didn't allow him as much freedom and independence as I did, so when push came to shove he'd rather live with me.

He was Robina's boy and I loved him. But where did he get his attitudes from? When Dr Mitra talked about 'frozen values' back in Delhi, one of the people I thought about immediately was Sunny. Whereas my parents' values were understandably frozen, because they had come from another country as adults and failed to integrate properly into their adopted home, Sunny's values were harder to comprehend. In a sense they were the same as my parents', and undeniably he had learnt much of what he believed from them. But in another way they were like some strange hybrid. He believed in keeping the women from his culture 'pure', and punishing those who threatened that ideal, but at the same time he wanted to enjoy all the freedoms that the UK culture offered young men like him.

'I would never marry a girl from England,' he would say when we argued.

'But you go out with girls from England all the time.'

'You might use them, yeah, if you wanted to, but decent girls are from India.'

He had a similar bizarre attitude to caste. Even though he had only ever been to India on holiday, he was immensely proud of the fact that he was a *jatt*. At Asian weddings in the UK, he would be one of the ones standing up and singing these traditional songs about how they're *jatts*, they're warriors, and so on. I would tell him that I didn't believe in the caste system, and most certainly not in the UK where it was completely alien and irrelevant.

'How can you say that?' he'd say. 'You're a *jatt*.'

'And what about Natasha?' I'd reply. He had no answer to that.

One day, out of the blue, Sunny said, '*Masi*, I want to meet my father.' That had been Robina's dearest wish, which she had passed on to me a week before she died. So we tracked down Navtej and we both went to visit him in Toronto. He had a business there running petrol stations and was doing well. I took Anna and Jordan with me, and we were given a royal welcome. Navtej had remarried, but he had never had another child. And here was Sunny, whom he'd last seen when he was a baby of six months, now a strapping eighteen-year-old of six foot four. Navtej said he'd love it if Sunny went to live with him in Canada. A year later, off he went.

It seemed like an ideal solution. Sunny wasn't happy living with me. Not only did he question my values, he questioned my right to campaign. Karma Nirvana was founded in 1994 and had got National Lottery funding in 1996, but it wasn't until after Dad died in 1999 that I really started to speak out in public. Sunny didn't approve. 'Why do you have to go on television and talk about all these things?' he'd ask. Then, 'Why do you have to talk about my mum? Can't you leave her out of it?'

'She was my sister,' I would reply. 'She died in a horrific way. And I want to speak about that.'

For him, I think, it was mainly embarrassment with his mates that his *masi* was doing all this, was not part of the traditional status quo.

A month or so after Sunny left for Canada I phoned to see how he was getting on. He said he was doing fine. But a few months after that I got another call. '*Masi*, please,' he said, 'come and get me. I can't live here.'

'What's happened?'

'Just come and get me.'

So I dropped everything and went. When I got to Toronto it was soon apparent that Sunny was having to live the same restricted life that we had experienced growing up with my parents. He worked day and night in one of Navtej's petrol stations. When he had any free time he wasn't allowed out on his own. If he even went to the gym he had to ask for money. He wasn't allowed to drink or smoke. He wasn't allowed to associate with white or black people, he was supposed to spend time only with his 'own people'. 'Now they're talking about wanting to arrange my marriage,' he said, 'I can't cope with it.'

So we all sat down and had a family meeting to discuss Sunny's future. Navtej and his wife weren't happy that I'd come over in the first place.

'You can't just turn up here and talk about taking him back to the UK,' they said.

'I'm only doing what he asked. To be honest with you, he's unhappy.'

'How dare you tell us he's unhappy? You haven't been here. You don't know what's been going on.'

'I didn't use the word, he did.'

The meeting rapidly turned into a furious row. Before long, all the old insults came tumbling out again. 'You disgraced your family, you married a *chamar*, you're no better than a prostitute. You've contaminated his mind now, you hussy, with your awful ways . . .'

I wasn't sticking around to hear that kind of thing, so we packed our bags and left. We had to lock ourselves in a room upstairs, grab all our things, find Sunny's passport and make a sharp exit. As we were leaving the house Navtej and his wife were calling me all the names under the sun, telling me what they really thought of me. I got Sunny into the hire car and scarpered.

Back home in England, Sunny came to live with me again. I thought after that experience he might have changed. And he did for a short while. He apologised to Natasha for the way he had been before; he even said to me, 'I understand now what Asian girls go through.' But he was soon back to his normal self. He started looking at me critically again, shouting at me in my own home and calling me a runaway.

I decided it was about time he had his own place. After all, he had the money. So I helped him find a flat and set it up. The next thing I knew he was living with a girl I had introduced him to, one of the young women we had helped at Karma Nirvana. I'd invited her to my house for Christmas dinner as she had nowhere to go and I felt sorry for her. She met Sunny there and soon formed a relationship. I was quite proud of Sunny to start with; perhaps, I thought, his experience in Canada had got him to rethink his values. But then after a while it became apparent that he wasn't treating her well. He was very controlling. He would insult her and call her a runaway, too.

She ended up confiding in me about him. 'He doesn't respect me,' she said. 'He calls me names. He says I'm not what he would call "marriage material".'

So he hadn't changed. I felt sorry for her and for him, but it wasn't for me to get involved. In the end she left him because she didn't see a proper future with him. He was soon on the phone to me, telling me that her leaving him was all my fault. 'You got right into her head, didn't you? Got her to think in your white ways, your English ways.'

'No, Sunny. You haven't treated her well.'

'Why can't you keep your nose out of it?'

'You met her at my house. She came to me for support, so of course I'm going to offer her that.'

He ended up screaming abuse at me down the phone. I was in the office at Karma Nirvana and there were two other women in there with me, my friend and colleague Shazia and another of the volunteers, who couldn't help but hear every word. 'You're a whore,' he was yelling, amid a blizzard of expletives, 'a prostitute, a runaway. Why don't you . . . ?' I shan't repeat his obscene invitation, but my colleagues were shocked that he'd dared say such a thing to his *masi*, however little he respected her. That was the last time I spoke to him. I couldn't carry on after that.

About a year later I was in Debenhams in Derby. It was Christmas and I was shopping with Anna when we both saw him across the floor, looking at shirts in the men's department.

'Oh, Mum,' Anna said, 'look, there's Sunny *paaji*.' *Paaji* means brother.

'I said, "I know, darling."'

'Let's go and say hello.' She was only eleven, bless her.

So I walked over to him and I said, 'Hello, Sunny, how are you?'

He looked at me blankly, as if my daughter and I were total strangers. 'What?' he said.

'Hi, *paaji*,' Anna was saying sweetly.

'Let's let bygones be bygones,' I said. 'Anna spotted you and wanted to say hello.'

'Fuck off. The pair of you.'

And he walked off. Just like that. Anna and I just looked at each other. It was me who started to cry. 'Come on,' I said, 'Let's go.'

'That wasn't very nice, Mum, was it?'

'No, it wasn't very nice, Anna. But never mind, it's done, let's go.'

That was the last time we saw each other; I've never heard from him since. I find it sad. Not only is he Robina's only son, but my father left me in trust to help him with his life.

I remember such happy times with Sunny when he was growing up. When we first lived as a family together in Warwick Avenue, I would get him to help with the chores, and his particular job was fluffing up the sofa cushions, because he was so big and strong. He used to go at them with his fists as if they were punchbags and they came up great. He was good at hoovering too and was thrilled if you told him he'd done a good job. He always joined us at the table for meals.

Then I remember going jogging with him around Derby. 'You'll never beat me,' he would say, turning on his heel, as he paced easily along just a few yards ahead of me. I didn't either. I watched him grow up, have his first drink, experiment with cigarettes, the works. When he was eighteen I bought him a white linen suit. It was hard to find because he's such a big guy that getting his size wasn't easy. But he was so over the moon about it, grinning from ear to ear as he went off to another Asian wedding.

The last I heard of him through the grapevine was that Ginda may be arranging his marriage. I'm sure he will end up finding a nice girl from the Punjab, a *jatt* just like him, who will have no understanding of the place she's going to. I imagine he can have his pick of the crop. From the perspective of someone out here in India, he has everything going for him. He can be the biggest peacock in the pride.

Back at the Jalandhar Country Inn we find the other Sunny in my life and what a joy it is to see him. My future son-in-law Anup is in his early twenties, a couple of years older than Natasha, a switched-on young man with a warm, laid-back manner and an easy smile. Tony and I shower and change and meet him in one of the hotel's two restaurants for a curry. Anup tells us about his flight, Birmingham to Amritsar via Turkmenistan, packed with UK Punjabis heading to India for business or pleasure. I am glad I was not on that flight. I would have been suspicious about every teenaged girl on the plane.

So now there is no more putting it off. Tomorrow morning we are going in to Kang Sabhu. We know where it is, how many inhabitants it has, how many are literate, even how many are involved with agriculture. If we'd stuck around in the Jalandhar Development Office a bit longer we could probably have come away with a detailed breakdown of all the castes too. Now we have to bite the bullet and see how they will receive me, the disowned daughter of the village.

We sit up quite late in the bar, discussing strategy. When we arrive in the village, should we all get out of the car at once? Or should Tony, the white man, stay in the vehicle for a bit, so we don't draw undue attention to ourselves? 'If it all kicks off,' he says, 'I can be out there in a flash.'

Of the three of us, Anup is the most relaxed about it all. If Kang Sabhu is a typical Punjabi village, he says, there should be a central street or square, where there will be shops and people hanging out who will be able to help us. Once the word gets out that I am looking for a long-lost sister, Anup reckons that people will just appear out of the woodwork. We don't have to tell them that I am a disowned woman who married across caste, a crime sometimes punishable by death in this and the neighbouring province. The objective is to find Bachanu. How she will react when her half sister is sprung on her out of the blue is her business. For what it's worth, Anup thinks she will be too curious not to receive me.

9

That night I hardly sleep at all. My stomach is churning and I'm lying there in my big hotel bed thinking: tomorrow is the day I meet my sister and finally find out whether I am to be accepted; or whether my father was right, shame really does travel and I am to be turned away. In the panicky small hours I imagine Bachanu standing there, hands up, eyes scornful. 'Don't come near me, I don't want to know.' The fact is, I have simply no idea what my family have told her about me over the years. Then again, perhaps they've told her nothing, or I am a subject that is never referred to, or maybe she even thinks I'm dead, just as my school friend Habiba Ahmed did when I met her at that bus stop in Derby.

It's such a huge day for me, but for Bachanu it will be starting just like any other. As I pull myself from my hotel bed and cross the room to the shower, I'm thinking: now Bachanu is waking up, washing, doing her morning chores, with no idea that her unknown sister is about to pay her a surprise visit.

I don't manage to eat much breakfast and am silent as we make for the car. Inder is discreet and professional as ever; a polite smile, a quiet good morning, then he noses the Toyota out from the hotel forecourt into the chaotic jostle of traffic. I watch his dark eyes skimming from left to right in the mirror, forever watching for a stray rickshaw or moped pushing in on his blind corner.

Anup and Tony have picked up on my mood. After all our discussions last night about how we're going to play it when we get to Kang Sabhu, they're quiet this morning. We make our way slowly through the busy traffic of central Jalandhar and turn left on the road to Nakodar, which is crowded on both sides with shops selling anything and everything. By a half-finished concrete apartment block, a stray dog noses among colourful piles of rubbish. A guy talking on a mobile phone spits out a stream of white *lassi* into the dust. On a roadside cart under a crimson parasol a pile of oranges is so neatly stacked up it's geometrical.

The clutter of commerce thins. Open country appears to left and right. In a green field of turnips a man in an orange shirt bends to hoe. 'MBD Books and Examination Master' says a big sign out on its own. On the right is a pottery, mugs and jugs and plates and pots laid out for sale; on the left, in the shade of a tall eucalyptus, a stall sells colourful inflatable children's toys. On the opposite side of the road, turbaned men on mopeds race past. Yellow turbans, green turbans, blue turbans, pink turbans. Is one of them a relative of mine? Will one of them, later, be part of an angry group that throws me out of the village?

Now we are getting into a built-up area. More shop
fronts flash by. Sunny Light and Sound. Ghai Biscuits.
Glory Novelty Trading Company. Among the fruit and veg
stalls I spot old women, heads covered in shawls, buying
their groceries, gossiping. Could one of them be my sister?
Maybe we'll get to her house and there'll be no rejection
because Bachanu won't be in. I feel relieved at this thought,
even though I know it's absurd. I have come all this way to
try and see her.

We're back into open country, not there yet. The orange
canopy of an Indian Oil petrol station is on the left, then a
workshop selling windows; on the right a bus stop is
covered in Punjabi graffiti. Now we're into another built-
up area. Maa Burga Electronics. Lala Medicine Centre.
Kang Telecom.

Anup speaks to Inder and the car slows. My heart turns
over. This tatty row of shops is a far, far cry from what my
father described to me when I was a child, but we must be
here. This is it. Kang Sabhu in 2010.

'There's usually like a big entrance gate to the village,'
says Anup. Even as he's speaking, we all see it, on the left,
in the middle of the commercial strip, a tall, wide, square
arch painted in primrose yellow, pink and blue, its pediment decorated with large, neat Punjabi script. I only know
Punjabi to speak, not to read, so these symbols mean nothing to me.

Inder pulls the Toyota into the roadside. 'Shall I drive
in?' he asks.

Anup turns from the front seat to look at me and I nod.
'OK,' he says.

The car turns left, through the arch, and down into a dusty, brick-paved street, balconied houses to left and right. The street widens into a little square, a few shops on the left side. The two in the middle are closed with pull-down steel shutters. On the white wall above the one on the right is painted JOHAN TAILOR, LADIES & GENTS; the little store on the left is no more than a narrow opening in a salmon-pink wall on which is scrawled, in roughly painted black letters, STD and on the other side, PCO.

We stop the car and climb out. From outside Johan Tailor, two men are watching us. One stands, arms folded; the other sits in a big wheelchair that looks as if it has been put together out of old bicycles, with a green canvas back. Under his smart white shirt and dark waistcoat he has no legs. And what are *they* seeing? An Asian woman in a turquoise and cream *salwar kameez*, with a younger Asian man and a large, burly white fellow. What are they thinking? Here are some visitors from abroad: the UK, or Canada, or the US, come back to see their old village, maybe build a big new house with a fancy watertank . . .

Inside the smaller shop I glimpse two old ladies in head shawls. One sits on a white plastic chair talking to the other, who's up on a stool behind a narrow counter on which stand jars of sweets. Above her, brightly coloured rows of snack packets and household items are strung from a central wooden pole. 'Glory Snax' reads one string. 'King Scrubbers' says a card full of wire wool. A child's bicycle is propped up against the wall to the left.

Instinctively, I turn towards the old ladies, the *bibis*, as we used to call them at home. Here as there a *bibi* is a truly Asian character: someone who will know everything about a place and everyone in it. In a village like this they will know who lives here, who recently passed away, what girl got married and to whom – they are the primary source of gossip and information.

I walk up two concrete steps into the shop and say hello. '*Sat sri akal*.'

'*Sat sri akal*,' the old ladies reply, looking up.

'Where are you from?' asks the woman on the white plastic chair; she can tell instantly that I'm not local.

'The UK,' I say.

'I thought so.' She smiles. She has a brother in Derby, she says.

'In Derby,' I say. 'That's where I'm from.' We're laughing at the coincidence, but I'm also suddenly nervous. Perhaps, I think wildly, they will know about me already; but there's no point trying to cover up now.

The *bibi* is telling me her brother's name and the names of his children, Baljit and Daljit. Good Sikh names, I'm thinking, but I don't know the family. Why should I? There are thousands of Asian people in Derby. But now I feel as if I'm much closer to finding my sister. I'm in Kang Sabhu and here already is a family who have connections in Derby.

As we chat on I can see them both uncoiling like springs. One does the talking while the other one watches, eyes bright. Now they want to know all about me. I tell them I've never been to India before. I'm here to look for my sister, I say.

'*Hai rabba!*' she goes. 'Oh my God! You've got a sister and you've not met her? How can this be? We must find her for you.'

She starts talking excitedly to her friend. I've told them my name and now they're going from name to name among the families in the village, trying to work out who I could possibly be related to.

I turn and run back to the car. Tony and Anup are standing there watching.

'How's it going?' asks Anup.

'I need those photos.'

I grab the sheaf of family photographs from the back seat and bring them back. 'Why didn't you say you had photographs?' the ladies cry, snatching them up eagerly. 'Let's have a look.'

Other old women have appeared, magically, from nowhere. They're all wearing the same outfit: an oblong shawl wrapped round their heads and over their shoulders, beneath that a thick cardigan over their *salwar kameez*, though it's already as warm in the morning sunshine as on an English summer's day. On their feet they all have identical blue flip-flops.

The photos are passed round, amid much muttered speculation. I show them the picture of Bachanu standing against the tractor. 'Bachanu, Bachanu,' they repeat. They're saying it rings a bell, but no more than that. Then we come to a picture of my mother. She's grinning on the sidelines at a party, somewhere in India because it's outside and there are Indian relatives all around. I think it must have been Sunny's birthday, because there's a big cake on a table in the middle and my nephew is blowing candles out.

Bingo! Straight away the first *bibi* recognises her. She says my mother's name – Jagir Kaur. Now she can find someone in the village to help, she says. She names three particular aunties who might know more. As she hurries off, the old woman behind the counter smiles at me. 'Don't worry,' she says. 'We'll find your sister.'

I can hardly believe it. We've only been here five minutes and already someone recognises my mother. I am starting to believe that we really might find my sister. Now, one by one, these new aunties start appearing. They study the photos and shake their heads. No, sorry, they can't help. By this stage the group is about twenty strong and has moved off into the middle of the little square, where Tony and Anup have joined them. A man in a purple turban pitches up on a moped. Two teenaged lads crane in. A gaggle of children run over and dart away again, laughing. The whole village is going to know about us soon.

Then, suddenly, there's a light bulb moment. The gathered *bibis* have thought of someone who will know about my family. One of them goes off to get this latest auntie and soon enough she appears, a tall middle-aged woman in a purple headscarf. She may not be as old as the others but she's definitely a *bibi* in the making. She knows everything and everyone, apparently. She takes the photos and inspects them, slowly, one by one. And yes, sure enough, she not only recognises my mother, she knows who Bachanu is.

'This is Chanan Singh's daughter,' she says to the gathered crowd. Chanan Singh, my father. The thing that makes them suddenly all remember him, the defining factor, is that he was married twice. Clearly people in the village don't marry twice very often. His first wife, she tells us, was bitten by a snake, then he married the younger sister – Jagir Kaur, my mother. I feel excitement rising: this was the story I was told as a child, that Bachanu's mother died of a snakebite.

'Your aunt still lives here in the village,' she says to me. 'One of these women will go and fetch her now.'

She speaks to one of the *bibis,* who hurries off, past Johan Tailor and down the side alley beyond.

I stand there, amazed, shaking my head slowly at Anup, who has been listening to all this. 'My aunt,' I say. 'Which aunt?'

'Your father's brother's wife. She lives here in the village. With her son.'

My father's brother's wife. I didn't even know my father's brother had a wife, let alone a son. All my mother ever told me about him was that he was *paagal*, mad. That he used to wander round the village, shouting, and people avoided him.

'And what about my sister – Bachanu?'

'I don't know about your sister. I don't think she lives in this village.'

Suddenly, the old lady who is apparently my aunt appears. She's just like the other *bibis*: brown shawl over her head, off-white *salwar kameez* with a curtain-like pattern of yellow and grey flowers, blue flip-flops. She makes a beeline for me, then grabs my arm with bony fingers. Three silver bangles jangle on her wrist.

'You're our daughter,' she says. She has a prominent nose and her brown eyes are bright and beady under thick grey eyebrows. Her skin is wrinkled like old parchment. Blanched white hair straggles out from under her shawl. In one ear she wears a big gold earring. She clasps me to her and, uncomfortable though it is, a strange relief floods through me. So I am not to be rejected. At least not by her, not yet. Then I wonder if she even realises who I am. 'Come on,' she says, 'you must come to our house, you're our daughter.'

My aunt is a determined old woman. She's got my arm

in a vice-like grip and is pulling me away from the crowd. 'Let her go,' she shouts to the others. 'She's one of ours.'

They back away. I'm definitely her property. Now she's telling me I look like Yasmin, my sister. 'I was sorry to hear that your father died,' she says. 'He was a good man, a very good man.' Then she starts calling me Susie.

'She's calling me Susie,' I tell Anup. 'That's what my family called me as a child.'

'Looks like she's your auntie all right,' says Anup.

'Don't abandon me.'

'We won't.'

I let her lead me off out of the square and down the narrow alleyway beyond Johan Tailor. Anup and Tony follow. An open drain runs by the dusty criss-cross brick-work underfoot. Overhead I notice KANG SAB scrawled up on a wall. As we walk along, my arm still firmly in my aunt's grip, she's asking me all these questions. Why have I never come to India before? Why hasn't she seen me? Where do I live? Who am I married to? How many children do I have?

My sisters Yasmin and Prakash come regularly to visit, she says. She calls Prakash 'Pashie' like the rest of the family do. They don't stay for long, she says, they just flit in and flit out. The last time they all came with my mother was for Lucy's wedding. But they never mention me. Why is that? 'It's a shame you've waited so long to come,' she says, 'because I'm not so well now. Your uncle died a few weeks ago and I've not been well since. I live on my own with Bobby, my son. Your cousin, you'll meet him in a moment.'

My cousin . . . my uncle . . . who has recently died. My head is spinning.

'Where is my sister, Bachanu?' I ask.

She stops in her tracks for a moment. 'Forget about her,' she says, 'she's dead.'

This is so blunt I can't take it in.

'What,' I hear myself mutter. 'When did she die?' I ask.

'6 years ago. Didn't they tell you?'

'No. They didn't. Did she live with you?'

'No. Bachanu didn't live in this village. She lived with her husband in another village.'

My sister is dead. Has been for 6 years. And nobody from my family ever told me. Even as shock hits me, I feel anger rising.

I turn to Anup and Tony, who are walking right behind us. 'She just said my sister is dead.'

'I heard that,' says Anup.

'Bachanu?' says Tony.

'Yes, she died 6 years ago apparently.'

We turn sharp right, down another alley, then right again before stopping in front of a heavy steel door set into the high wall. My aunt pushes in and we find ourselves in a sunny courtyard. There's a covered veranda to one side and doorways to darkened rooms beyond. Just out of the sun are a couple of black steel chairs and a daybed – a *manja* – on which lies a crumpled quilt printed with big blue flowers on a cream background.

Lurking further back in the shadows is a lanky man with thick, dark stubble, shot through with grey. He's wearing a black shell suit with white stripes over a crimson T-shirt;

on his head is a black baseball cap, which is reversed, so you can read the tiny logo: 'Polo Sport'. He's easily in his forties but he looks like a superannuated teenager and also, eerily, exactly like my brother Balbir, who is also nicknamed Bobby.

He comes forward. My aunt is telling him who I am. 'Susie. Your cousin.'

He nods and smiles. 'You look just like Yasmin,' he says.

'Your mother just said that. Lots of people say that to me.' I feel somehow reassured; I'm clearly not an imposter. Now Bobby is staring at me, mouth open.

'Are you shocked?' I ask. 'I'm sorry . . .'

'It's not shock. I'm happy,' he says in Punjabi. 'I never imagined this day would come. That a cousin I didn't know I had would come to our house.'

I sit down on one of the steel chairs with the old lady. There are no cushions and none is offered. Now my aunt is telling me all about the house. This was my father's father's house; it's been in the family for generations. When my father lived over here in Kang Sabhu with my mother, before he went to England, this is where he lived. This is the house my mother would have come to as a young bride.

She gestures around the little courtyard. 'Your father used to sleep there, under this veranda. Your mother was in that room, with the children. Your mother and I were both daughter-in-laws. We lived in this house together. We had happy times. This was where she stayed when your father left, before she joined him in England.'

I look slowly round, trying to take it all in.

'Did she want to go?' I ask.

'Oh yes, she was never worried about going to England, she was excited. Her father was sorry to see her go, though. Bai. Especially after he'd lost one daughter.'

Bai. That was the old man who came to visit us in Derby, who was always huddled round the electric fire. 'So Bai was my mother's father?'

'Yes. Bai Singh. Her family weren't from this village, but when your mother got married she came to live here, like me.'

It's hard for me to imagine the two families living here together; the house is so tattered and run down. The paint-work on the walls is peeling badly, the stone floor of the courtyard has two long cracks running across it. In the middle of the courtyard a big metal container of water stands by a smaller bucket and a lone soap dish.

'Your sisters come here all the time,' she says again.

'Do they help you?'

She smiles. 'They bring clothes. Now and again they give us a bit of money.'

I find myself wondering what they tell my aunt and my cousin when they're here. Do they know that Robina died, I ask. Yes, Bobby says. They heard she had committed suicide, but they didn't know how or why. They thought she was unhappy in her marriage.

'In her marriage,' I repeat slowly. 'Didn't you know she was married twice?'

'No.'

'She left her first husband and had a love marriage. They didn't tell you that?'

'No.'

But why am I surprised? These are the things that my family wouldn't have wanted them to know about over here.

I ask them about Lucy. Do they remember her wedding, (the wedding that should have been mine)? What was that like? Yes, Bobby tells me, he remembers it well. Lucy didn't want to get married.

'Did she tell you that?'

'No. But you could just tell. From the look in her eyes. She looked scared.'

'She didn't want to get married,' my aunt agrees. She's very frank, surprisingly so.

I look round the courtyard, imagining my sisters here. Walking through these doorways, sleeping in these rooms, being dressed up for weddings they didn't want to go through with. Even if they had wanted to run away, where could they have run to?

Nowhere, is the answer.

I want to know more about Bachanu. Is it really true that she's passed away, I ask.

Yes, says the old lady. Six years ago. She used to come here all the time, and then she didn't. But her husband Gurdial is still alive, and her children too. They live in a village not far from here, Aulka, beyond Nakodar. 'Didn't your sisters tell you she'd died?'

'No, they didn't.'

They didn't, Auntie, because they don't talk to me. Who am I to be informed if someone has died? My father was in hospital, none of them told me that. Robina committed suicide, none of them told me that. It's no surprise that they didn't tell me about my sister either, just a cruel reminder of the truth of my situation.

'My sisters ignore me,' I say. 'If they see me they refuse to talk to me. They don't even talk to my children.'

Bobby says nothing. My auntie nods sadly. 'If you can't talk to your brothers and sisters who *can* you talk to?' she says.

I decide it's time to tell them my story. Who knows, perhaps they already know more of it than I realise. 'I was the one who was supposed to marry that man that Lucy married,' I say. 'But I said to my mum and dad, "I don't want to get married, I want to go to school. I want an education." I ran away from home,' I continue, 'my family have disowned me for 29 years. I haven't spoken to Pashie or Yasmin for nearly thirty years.'

They're visibly shocked. I don't think that they did know about me, after all. Will they carry on talking to me? Is this the moment when I find out that their friendliness is conditional, that my father was only trying to protect me, that shame does travel?

'It's wrong,' says Bobby, slowly. 'Your father went to England. It's a Western culture. Your family should have accepted that you were going to integrate. If you wanted to say no to a marriage, that's fine. If you wanted to marry by choice, that's fine too. They're guilty, not you.'

I can hardly believe I'm hearing these words. 'So do you not look at me and think I've shamed you?' I ask.

'Not at all.'

'You don't think I've shamed my family?'

'No.'

'Because when I ran away from home, my mother said, "In our eyes, you're dead." Then, later, my father said I couldn't come to India, because I'd shamed them in England. And that if I came here that would somehow shame you too.'

Bobby shakes his head. 'That was wrong. It's a Western culture you live in. That's your life.'

'So what do you think of me now?' I ask.

'I think you did the right thing. You stood up for what you believed in. You didn't let yourself be forced to do something you didn't want.' He looks over at Anup and Tony. 'I think you're great,' he adds in English, with a big soft smile.

I am shaking my head in quiet amazement. That a member of my family should say such things to me! Anup has been listening to all this, but I want Tony to hear it, too. I call him over and repeat what Bobby has said, in English.

'So in a nutshell,' Tony says. 'Shame travels from West to East, but it doesn't seem to travel from East to West.'

'You were born in England,' says Bobby in English, look-ing over at Tony. 'You have to follow Western culture.'

'If my mother and father were alive,' I ask in Punjabi, 'and they told you my story, what would you say to them?'

'We would tell them that they're guilty,' says Bobby.

'For thirty years,' I say, 'I've been made to feel guilty.'

'I tell you, you're great,' Bobby repeats in English.

Auntie has said nothing throughout all of this but she's been nodding along, repeating '*acha*', the Punjabi version of an approving 'mm'. For me to see and hear this is absolutely incredible. Acceptance. From members of my family. I never thought I'd live to hear that. Ever.

I'm half expecting tea or a drink to be brought, but nothing comes. We look through the rest of my photographs. I show them the picture of me receiving an honorary degree from Derby University. I am wearing a red cloak, trimmed with black. On my head is a soft black academic hat. My children – and Anup – are all around me. 'You're the intelligent one in the family,' Bobby says. 'You've educated yourself. That's great.'

I tell them about my children. 'That's why I wanted to make this journey,' I say, 'because they know nothing about their heritage. I want them to know they've got family here.'

This is the speech I should have been making to Bachanu, my sister. But I've left it too late. I should have done this years ago. Why did I wait?

I gesture across at Anup, sitting there with us, and tell them about Natasha, and how the pair of them are going to be married next year. One of the reasons he made this journey was so we could be sure my sister would accept me. Surely she wouldn't turn away the future son-in-law? Now it doesn't seem to matter.

'It would mean a lot to me,' I say, 'for her to know her family.'

'Invite me to the wedding then,' says Auntie and we all laugh.

'She's old,' Bobby says, 'she wouldn't be able to come.' But he could, he adds; and there is a definite gleam in his eye.

I ask if either of them have ever been to England.

They laugh. 'No,' says Bobby.

'Didn't any of my sisters ever invite you over?'

'We've asked them to call us over,' says Auntie. 'But none of them have.'

'Your sisters always say it's very hard to get a visa,' says Bobby.

We leave it there. I don't want to get drawn into making promises I can't keep. I'm still coming to terms with the existence of these two relatives of mine I didn't even know I had. Bobby reminds me so much of my brother Balbir. He even has his mannerisms: in particular, a way of scratching his chin with his hand.

'When you see them again, are you going to tell my sisters that I came here?' I ask.

'Yes,' Bobby says. 'We'll tell them.'

We talk more about the family, about Pashie. Do they know about her second husband Gurmal and his other wife over here in India? It turns out that they do. I tell them that Prakash's middle son, Ranjit, known in the family as Gugsy, is the one member of my family I do talk to. Like me, he was disowned, because he married a girl from a lower caste.

They didn't know that.

Bobby shakes his head. 'Caste doesn't matter,' he says. 'None of that should matter any more.'

That's a stark contrast to how my family and others feel in England, and not just in my and my parents' generation. My nephew Sunny is not the only young man who stands up at weddings and sings proud songs about being a *jatt*.

You see these car number plates, too, around Derby and Bradford and Leeds, which say things like JATT 1. To say nothing of the caste-based *gurdwaras*.

Now Bobby and his mother show us round the house. It's quite a big place and I start to imagine it as it must have been in my father's day, clean and comfortable, not semi-derelict as it is now. In the tiny kitchen off the courtyard there is just one blackened double cooking ring, next to an orange gas bottle on the floor against the wall. Metal dishes, like the ones Mum used to bring back from her trips, are stacked anyhow on the shelves above, along with cups and battered plastic bottles. The bedroom behind the veranda must once have been a lovely room, with its wooden doors and shutters on its two big windows. But now it's a mess, with one bedstead in the middle of the room on which lies a grubby brown rug. Another up against the wall is stacked with miscellaneous junk: a mirror, an iron, a school exercise book, an old jacket, a heap of colourful plastic bags. Grey plaster fills the cracks in the old pink paint on the walls.

The rooms on the other side of the yard are in a similar state. There are more bedsteads empty or piled with junk. A lovely old wooden chest with square drawers is pushed into a corner, crumpled newspapers and a chapatti pan lie on top of it. Calendars and cards are tacked up anywhere on the peeling walls. There's a poster of Jesus, too, in orange robes, just along from one of the later Sikh gurus. My mother would never have allowed that while she was living here. She even hated the fact that Ginda sometimes took us kids to Sunday school.

'That's my faith,' I say to Bobby and he smiles.

'Sikhs respect all faiths,' he replies. 'God is one – and everywhere.'

It's such a contrast to the attitudes I was brought up with at home.

Out the back there's another yard, with weeds springing up in the cracks of the brick floor. A weather-beaten ladder stands against the peeling paint of the wall. A towel and an old pair of red shorts hang on a single clothes line.

'This is the house your dad lived in,' my aunt says. I wonder whether she might be suffering from some kind of dementia, as she keeps repeating what she's told me before. She used to live here, she goes on, with him and my mother. They never fought. My father was a good man, a happy man. When he went to England he went with several others from this village. He wanted a better life. For him and his children . . .

Bobby points out a *manja* propped up against a wall, its four wooden feet poking out into the courtyard. Its criss-cross webbing only covers three quarters of the frame. 'This was the *manja* your father used to like to sit on, when he was here,' he says. 'He used to sit on it at night, talking and drinking *desi*. I think he was happy there.'

'Is there a big tree in the village?' I ask. 'That Dad might have sat under on other evenings? When he was younger?'

'There's a tree on his land,' Bobby says. 'I don't know whether he ever sat under it, but it's quite big.'

'His land?'

'The land he used to farm, before he went to England. Would you like to see it?'

Of course we would! It's on the edge of the village. Bobby says he'll show us.

We say goodbye to my aunt, promising to return later today or tomorrow, and Bobby leads us back down the alleyway to the square. He gets into the Toyota with us and we drive out and along the busy main road for a hundred yards or so before turning left through another arch onto a dirt track that separates the main village from the fields beyond. A quarter of a mile down here there's a rough track off to the right which the car can't manage, so we pile out and follow Bobby across this land, which is divided into oblong plots, perhaps thirty by eighty yards each, separated by low ridges with a ditch between them. Three of these, Bobby explains, belonged to my grandfather. They passed down to his father and my father. Now he has two of them and my sister Prakash has the other, the one at the bottom, which she leases out. This field we are coming to now, covered with the flattened yellow stalks of a recently harvested crop of rice, was the land my father would have farmed.

At the far end of the strip is a broken down brick cowshed, with no roof, and wooden doors falling into each other. Standing around it, providing shade from the midday sun, is a copse of trees. One is indeed much bigger than the others. A *peeple* tree, Bobby says. Looking at it, five trunks intertwined, spreading upwards into a mass of branches and dark green leaves, I am certain, in my gut, that this is the tree my father told me about as a child.

I feel a great rush of emotion. This is it, the very place where Dad would have sat talking in the evening with the

other men; where, in the heat of the day, his bullocks would have found shade from the sun. I stand under it and reach out to touch the strong, smooth trunk, look up at the leaves shifting and rustling in the warm midday breeze.

I turn away from the others. Suddenly I am in tears. I long for my father to be here with me now. Why couldn't he have brought me back with him to Kang Sabhu? Why did he think that the shame he and my mother felt and were made to feel in Derby would travel back here? When as far as I can understand from the conversation I've had this morning, it seems that my family here, my Indian family, don't care about what I did at all.

I feel robbed. I should have been here with Dad. It should have been him explaining this place to me, to my children too, with that familiar smile on his face, not some cousin I didn't even know I had. To have missed coming to India with him because of some decision I made in my life, just feels so wrong.

But even as I stand here, holding the trunk of this tree, with tears streaming down my cheeks, looking out across the patchwork of fields stretching away on the flat, fertile plain, a new feeling comes over me – of a strange kind of reassurance. Because it was all true, wasn't it? Everything he told me was true. Now I can see what Dad saw, day in, day out, as he worked the land. At one level I can imagine him being content with this, with his bullocks and his cows and his life as 'the village milkman'. But at another level, it wasn't enough. He had dreams of something more. As my aunt told me this morning, he had an idea of a better life, not just for himself, but for his children. For me. And I'm grateful for that, because if he hadn't gone to England, my life would have been very different. I wouldn't be who I am.

The shame is that when they went to the UK, and settled there, my parents didn't embrace the values and culture of their new home. Back in Delhi, Dr Mitra said it. Here, this morning, Bobby repeated it. 'You live in a Western world, Jasvinder. You're bound to want an education, to integrate, to do as you want to do, to choose your partner.' It wasn't my choice to be born in England. From the very moment that Dad decided to leave this place, to make a new life in another country, he should have embraced that new life totally, for himself and for us, his children. Clinging onto values and customs that had nothing to do with the world he had moved to has caused so much hurt.

My sadness is changing to anger and a new conviction. If my mother and father were alive today, I would go back to them, having done this trip, and I would say, 'But Mum, Dad, your own family think it's OK to be in England, and to integrate, and to have aspirations. Who are you trying to prove to that it's not? These people here aren't bothered, so who is? Is it the Asian community in the UK? Because if so, what's that all about?'

I am going to take this experience back home and it's going to make me so much stronger as a campaigner. I'm really going to get out there and give this message to those members of the Asian community stuck with their frozen values in the past. 'You lot are living in cloud-cuckoo land,' I'm going to tell them, 'because it's not the people over here, in India, that you're convincing that you're these good, honourable human beings you think you are – they really don't care. So allow your children to be British Asians. Embrace the culture. Let them get on with it and trust them.'

There's one final thing, something that I realise, as I turn away from the tree at last, that has been staring me in the face all along. People often ask me, at conferences and meetings and such like, 'Why are you different? What made you stand up and resist the shackles that were being forced on you?' Now I can see the answer. I got that rebellious spirit from my father. It was always there.

I look away from the dark shifting leaves and up into the empty blue sky. 'Dad, are you watching me,' I murmur. 'Bless you, Dad.'

Anup and Tony are on the other side of the cowshed, playing with four small boys who have appeared from nowhere. Four identical dark moptops with different coloured T-shirts: blue, red, orange and yellow. Cavemankids Champions reads the blue one; SPEED say contrasting letters of green, pink and blue on the orange shirt, above a logo of a man on a big motorbike. The boys line up to leap from the top of the cowshed, landing with shrieks on the hard ground below. Then they yell with delight as they swing from the lower branches of one of the trees. I remember Dad telling me about one of the village boys who climbed up into the branches of his tree 'like a monkey' to put a rope high up, so the other kids could also get up there. It would have been a young lad just like these.

Everything has changed in Kang Sabhu: trucks and cars and mopeds race past on the busy tarmac main road. The shops sell mobile phones and videos as well as fruit and vegetables and garments and haircuts. Yet in another way, out here in the warm shade, with these boys leaping around, things are much the same. Tony lines them up for a photo, then Anup asks them what they want to be when they grow up. One wants to be a doctor. Another a policeman. Tony is a policeman, we tell them, and they look at him with new awe.

Anup and Tony lead on, back down the dusty track towards the car. Ahead of us, across the fields, the white onion-shaped cupola of the *gurdwara*, capped with its bright, cone-like helmet of gold, rises above the rest of the village; not far to its right, another huge expat mansion is going up, red brick and grey concrete, dwarfing the other more modest dwellings the locals live in.

As we arrive at the narrow tarmac road that skirts Kang Sabhu, Bobby is greeted by an old man on a bicycle. Under his dark blue turban he has shrewd brown eyes surrounded by laughter lines; below, the thick white moustache and long white beard of all the Sikh elders. He greets me with a *namaste*.

'*Sat sri akal.*'

'*Sat sri akal.*'

'I know that you are a daughter from here,' he says to me in Punjabi, 'but I can't place you. I'm also wondering who this big white man is with you. And this other gentleman.'

'A friend from the UK,' I tell him. 'And my future son-in-law. My father was Chanan Singh.'

'Chanan Singh.' He breaks into a big grin. 'I knew your

father.' He clasps his hands together and shakes his head. 'Your father was my best friend. He was a good man, a very good man.'

He's just saying that, is my first thought. Here we are, visitors from the UK, and like the nice old man we met yesterday he just wants to be part of it all. But as we continue talking it becomes clear he did know both my parents well. My father first went to England in 1951, he tells me. He went by boat from Bombay and it took him two weeks. He went for five years initially, then came back. He stayed for two more years in Kang Sabhu, before he finally left with my mother and the three children. I wonder whether maybe his decision to go to the UK wasn't that simple, given that it took the family two years to go. Maybe

Mr Singh and I.

he had doubts about exchanging all that he knew here: friends, family, life in the fields under a hot sun, for the alien world of Derby: the cold, the night shifts, the crowded, unwelcoming city.

The old man's name is Kurnail Singh. He is 74, ten years younger than my father would have been, if he were here with us now. They grew up together. They were like brothers, he says. 'Please come to my house,' he asks now. 'It's just up here. It would be an honour for me. And I'll tell you more about your father.'

That's enough for me. Today I am going to take up such offers. We follow him up the road for a couple of hundred yards and come to his house, which looks straight out over these very fields. Up steep stairs to a room where sunlight falls onto a double bed through narrow windows covered with ornamental metal grilles. Here we sit, Kurnail Singh and I, in a filigree of shadow, on a quilt with a bright pattern in turquoise, crimson and cream. To one side is a vase of chrysanthemums, yellow and orange.

An elderly woman appears from a side room in a cream *salwar kameez*, then a younger woman in a pink shawl. There's a young girl too, perhaps eleven or twelve years old, who stands to one side, in a knee-length crimson dress over crimson trousers; she smiles nervously and fingers her long dark ponytail. Anup, Tony and Bobby are offered dark moulded plastic chairs. The younger woman brings a tray of glasses of Coca-Cola and places it carefully on a low table in the centre of the room. The girl follows soon after with two plates of warm samosas.

I bring out the sheaf of photos from my bag and show

them to Kurnail. He takes the little black and white one of my father with 'May 1958' stamped on the back, which must have been a passport photo. It shows a good-looking young man with dark hair swept off his forehead and cut short above his ears, who gazes out proudly at the camera. He is wearing a collarless white shirt and a thin suit jacket, the shoulders and lapels of which are just visible.

'There he is,' he says, shaking his head. 'He had a beautiful face.' He was a very special man, he adds. He stood out. 'He was bold,' he continues, 'nothing ever scared him. He was always ahead of everyone else in the village, he was even the first to get an earring. Everyone wanted to be like him, me included.' Kurnail smiles and nods to himself and for a few moments, watching him, his long white beard and his wrinkles vanish, and I see the clear bright eyes of a young boy, looking up at a teenager he admired. I think of my son, Jordan, back home in Yorkshire, and wonder how much of Dad's spirit he has inherited, intelligent and ambitious young lad that he is.

'Your grandfather, too, Bucha Singh, was a highly respected man in this village. He was known as someone whom the poor people could always go to for help.'

'So he wasn't poor himself?'

'No, Bucha Singh wasn't poor. He used to buy and sell cattle. But he always used what extra he had to help good causes.'

I feel both excited and proud as I sit here. Before this trip I knew nothing about my grandparents, on either side. Now I know who Bai was, and I'm hearing that my father's father was a substantial figure who helped people, much as I try and do in my work.

Kurnail writes out my grandparents' names for me: Bucha Singh was my father's father, his wife was Bishem Kaur. Then, above that, he writes *Dila Singh*. That was his father, my great-grandfather. As for my father and his brother Naranjan, the two sons were very different in character, Kurnail says. My father wasn't interested in being educated beyond a certain point. He was ambitious, he wanted to get out into the world and work. That's why he went to England. Naranjan was less ambitious; he was happy to stay in the village.

We have come to the photo of me receiving my honorary degree.

'These are my children,' I tell Kurnail. 'Natasha, that's the eldest one. She's going to marry Sunny here.' I bring in Anup with a gesture. 'Then this one is Anna. And the youngest one, Jordan.'

Kurnail looks from me to Anup and back again. 'She is a beautiful girl.'

'Yes, she is.'

'You are a lucky man. And the others are beautiful, too.'

Now Kurnail looks over at Tony.

'And who is your husband?' he asks.

It is time to tell Kurnail my story. I go over everything: how I ran away, married a man from a different caste, how my family disowned me. He listens quietly until I've finished. Then he nods.

'You were born in England,' he says. 'So you can do anything you want to do.' There is silence for a few seconds, then he adds, 'People in England can achieve anything.'

We have finished our Coke and the plate of samosas. Kurnail suggests we move upstairs. We follow him, his wife, the younger woman and the little girl. Two floors up we come to a little terrace. There are chairs, a low table to one side and a big satellite dish at one end. Over the parapet wall at the end there's a fine view back over the village. Directly beneath us are a few small square domestic plots, planted up with the green leaves of turnips and radishes, just like my father's allotment in Derby. A broad-leaved fig tree stands against a crumbling brick wall, next to a pink flowered frangipani. Hens cluck down dirt paths, between pots overflowing with herbs. Behind that are a couple of neat new houses, expat dwellings doubtless, though not as big as the ones we saw on the GT Road, with the fancy watertanks. In the other direction are the fields. Strips of ploughed-up earth alternate with the bright green of a new crop and the faded yellow of a harvested field. One long oblong of sugar cane has attracted a flock of parakeets, which swoop and dive, green wings fluttering. Even from up here you can hear their squawks. Further away a man carries a pile of straw on his shoulders along one of the raised dykes of earth between the fields. Beyond him, off in the middle distance, I can see my father's land: the *peeple* tree standing tall above the copse around the broken down cowshed.

'Your grandfather used to sit under that tree and drink the *desi* he had made,' says Kurnail, confirming everything.

'My dad used to make *desi* at home in Derby. In his shed in the garden. I remember finding him out there at three in the morning with some friends of his. "Don't tell your mother," he said.'

Kurnail laughs. 'We have to make it secretly here as well. But your father used to like a drink. I remember that. When I was a little boy, your grandfather Bucha Singh would be sitting under that tree with his friends and he would shout at your father, "Come and join us." We would go over and sit on the *manja* with them. They would sit there all day.'

'Did you have a drink?'

'Oh yes. We all had a drink. And when he came back, twelve years ago, Chanan was exactly the same as he'd always been. Things never bothered him. He would never get angry about the things some people get angry about. He was a happy man. When you ran away, it was probably your mother who felt most strongly about the shame.'

'You're right,' I say. 'I think it probably was. My mother ruled the roost at home. My father would always be in the background.'

Kurnail smiles. 'When your father came back here,' he says, 'to me, it was as if he never left.' He had a son himself, he says, who went over to England. He was a hotel manager there, but then he became ill and died. This woman here, says Kurnail, gesturing at the younger woman, who stands watching silently from the end of the terrace, was his wife, and the girl in red is his daughter.

'Have they been to England?'

'No. He would come back and visit them here. But I have

a request for you. This little girl is twelve years old. Perhaps you could take her to England. Think of her future and take her back with you.'

He's completely serious and I'm taken aback. I have great respect for this friend of my father's, who has been so welcoming and hospitable. He has listened to and accepted my story totally, just as my aunt and cousin did. But I can't see myself suddenly deciding to adopt his granddaughter.

I smile at her. She is standing right by me and I wonder what she thinks. 'Do you want to go to England?' I ask.

She laughs, nervously. With her grandfather and mother right beside her what else is she going to do? What does she think England is? Does she have any idea of what it's really like? Normanton Road, Derby, as opposed to the warm winter sunshine of Kang Sabhu? Or does she just see the big houses springing up round her village, and all the other villages in the area, and think that England is a fabulous place where money grows on trees.

'How would you feel about her going to England?' I ask her mother. She has the same eyes as her daughter, dark as sloes. Her lips are pursed. She shrugs her shoulders and says nothing. I get the strong feeling that she would not like to see her daughter go.

After we've taken our leave from Kurnail Singh, we say goodbye to Bobby. He has been sitting to one side of the terrace on a *manja*, half taking in the conversation, half, it seems, in a world of his own. I find myself wondering about his life, how he's ended up here living in that house with his ailing mother, incongruously dressed like an American teenager. What happened to the marriage in New Zealand? Perhaps his resemblance to my brother extends to more than just mannerisms and a similar lost, roaming, hangdog quality he has. Despite them being teenage sweethearts, Balbir's marriage to Dawn didn't work out either, and they ended up divorced. A second marriage also failed; by this stage, my brother was an alcoholic. The last I knew of him was what I learnt from the front page of the *Derby Evening Telegraph*. He was being sent to prison for arson. He had been depressed, the report said, and tried to set his house on fire.

'So, shall we see you when we come back tomorrow morning?' I ask.

'Yes, I would like that . . .'

'D'you want to come with us in the car to Gurdial's house? Show us the way?'

He shrugs. 'That might be awkward,' he says. 'I haven't seen him for so many years. He might not even recognise me.'

'Would that matter?'

Bobby looks down at his trainers. 'I suppose I could come with you and stay in the car.'

'Why would you want to do that?'

'Maybe it would be best if you went on your own.'

I look over at Anup and he makes a face; there's something odd going on here.

It's not until the evening, back at the hotel in Jalandhar, that the truth of what has happened starts to sink in. It has been such an extraordinary day. I have finally made it to Kang Sabhu. My worst fears were not realised. There was nobody there to point the finger and tell me I was a shamed woman: 'Leave the village now!' I can almost laugh at the image I've been carrying in my head for all this time.

Better than that, I found some relatives I never knew I had. I was welcomed into the house where my father lived and grew up, where his father lived before him. I saw the land Dad farmed, the tree he told me about all those years ago. I met his old friend, Kurnail Singh, who told me how highly Dad was thought of in the village, and his parents too. My grandfather was a man of consequence who also had the time to help others.

But at the end of it all, I have to accept this now, there was no Bachanu. No sister to give me a tiny bit of immediate family to hold onto in my heart. Sadly, stupidly, I have left my trip too late. I should have done this years ago. I will never now be able to ask her all those questions I longed to ask. Then I think, 'Come on, Jasvinder. Things happen for a reason. Maybe you weren't meant to meet her.'

If I'm totally honest, almost the worst thing is that I wasn't told. From what I can gather from Bobby and my aunt, my sisters knew that Bachanu had died and they didn't let me know. I find that very hurtful. Once again it underlines the injustice of my situation, the way my family continues to treat me.

As I pace up and down my hotel room, I'm also wondering about Bobby. There was something very strange about the way he said goodbye this afternoon. I got the strong feeling that he and Gurdial have fallen out. Maybe it's all tied up with the land, because there was something that didn't add up about what he told me when we were out in the fields this afternoon. I find it hard to believe that Dad would have signed that lower field over to Prakash and not given Bachanu and her family anything. We will see Bobby again tomorrow, and hopefully find out more from Gurdial. But I'm a bit suspicious. There's even a part of me that thinks that Bobby might be on the phone to my sisters in England right now, telling them I'm here, asking about the story I told them. *'So she ran away from home, she says it was because she didn't want an arranged marriage, blah blah blah.'* All too easily I can imagine the conversation.

If Bobby has rung them, what will happen now? Surely, if they know I'm here, the next call my sisters are going to make is to Gurdial, reminding him exactly who I am and what I've done. Part of me has high hopes for tomorrow: that we will find Bachanu's husband, just as we found my aunt and cousin, and that he will welcome us. He will be happy to tell me more about my sister, there will be children of hers there for me to meet, my nephews and nieces. Maybe one of them will even look a bit like her. But another part of me fears that after the up of today, tomorrow I am going to get the down. In the photograph I have of him, with his high white turban, Gurdial looks like a stern and unbending character. I fear he may more censorious than Bobby or my aunt. My sisters will have got to him. He may even refuse to see me.

10

The following morning, we are back on the road to Nakodar. The same turbans on the same mopeds flash by on the opposite side of the road. I'm starting to notice familiar landmarks. The grey concrete of the half-finished apartment block. The big sign in the turnip fields. The cheery kids' stall with its colourful balloons and inflated toys. The orange canopy of the Indian Oil petrol station.

Today we're not stopping at Kang Sabhu. We've decided not to take Bobby with us to Aulka. It would be a squeeze in the car, and the truth is I'd rather face Gurdial on my own. If there is going to be some kind of rejection I don't want Bobby to witness it. Also, my cousin was being so weird about whether he should come or not. When Tony, Anup and I discussed it over supper in the hotel last night, we all got the feeling that maybe there's been some kind of fall-out with Gurdial. So we've arranged to see Bobby this afternoon, on our way back to Jalandhar. I want to say goodbye to my aunt before we go north and also look round Dad's house again. In any case, if things go well with Gurdial, maybe we'll understand more about what happened to Dad's land, and why Bobby was being the way he was.

'Kang Telecom' flashes by on the left. There's the arch to the village with its Punjabi-inscribed pediment. Lala Medicine Centre, Mahli Garments, Iqbal Digital Studio, Ajay Auto Works. It's a busy little place these days.

Beyond Kang Sabhu the land opens out again. The patchwork of fields stretches away in both directions. Some teenaged boys play cricket on a brown pitch. There's a strip of shacks by the roadside, piled up on each other, surrounded by litter. It's hard to believe that people can actually live in such squalid conditions. Then, on the other side, there's another gleaming mansion.

'Built in India, paid for in England,' says Anup.

Nakodar is a proper country town. Not as big as Jalandhar, but with streets packed with garment shops. Scarves and fabric seem to hang everywhere. It looks as if there's recently been some kind of festival going on, as the overhead telephone lines are hung with colourful triangular pendants and streamers.

Beyond, the countryside is emptier. I start to get the feeling that we are way out in the Punjab now. Inder follows our map down a little country road with trees on either side. Then another village looms up across the fields. 'This should be Aulka,' he says.

The entrance arch is taller than the Kang Sabhu one and is altogether grander, despite being stuck out here in the middle of nowhere. It's covered with white tiles on which is painted a bold pattern: red, yellow and blue flowers wind around green leaves and blue grapes, twining up to a pediment which is topped on each side by little towers, capped with onion-shaped cupolas. In the middle is a canopy with three arches, flanked on each side by long-necked blue peacocks.

Through the main arch, the village is the same mixture of obvious poverty and expat new build, though much crazier and more extravagant here than in Kang Sabhu. The big, brand new houses have those same jokey water tank sculptures up on their roofs that we saw on the GT Road: there's an aeroplane up on one house, a fat pigeon

Entrance to Aulka.

on another; another has a giant umbrella mounted on it. To the left, behind high white walls, is a huge mansion, three long storeys high, with wide terraces surrounding each storey, complete with battlements in white stucco, orange tile and black wrought iron. At the front, the big double gates have seriously fancy ironwork in black, white and gold with stars, flowers, wheels, curlicues. The curving top is decorated with gold *fleur de lys*; at each side black and orange pillars are topped with carriage lamps. Beyond, you get a glimpse of the neatly-planted gardens which surround the place.

But the main street is paved with the same dusty brick-work as at Kang Sabhu. Weeds push up in cracks. The off-white paint is peeling in great strips from the buildings on the left. An old bedstead is propped up against a wall to the right. To one side, by an open doorway, three women sit around on moulded plastic chairs, gossiping. They are well wrapped up. Heavy shawls cover their *salwar kameez*.

Inder parks the car and Anup, Tony and I get out. This time I already have my sheaf of photographs with me. As we approach the ladies, they get to their feet.

'*Sat sri akal*,' I say, in greeting.

'*Sat sri akal*.'

'This is Aulka?'

'Yes, this is Aulka.'

'We're looking for a man who we think lives in this village, or nearby. His name is Gurdial Singh. He was married to a woman called Bachanu, who died a few years ago. She was my sister. But we think Gurdial still lives here somewhere with their children.'

In the time it takes to say this, several other women have materialised from nowhere. Suddenly we have a group of six or seven women, one of whom is carrying a child. As I hand out my photographs, they all crane in to have a look. One is of Bachanu with the tractor, the other of Bachanu with Gurdial. The chatter level rises. The name Bachanu is repeated, amid much nodding. Then they are all grinning, as if at a huge private joke.

'This is Bachanu,' says a woman in a blue shawl with a prominent gap in her front teeth, pointing at the photograph.

'Yes.'

'She's not dead. She lives with her husband on a farm just over there.'

The others are all nodding and pointing with the flat palms of their hands. 'She lives over there,' says another. 'She's alive.' 'Just over there,' they chorus.

Anup is grinning. I turn to Tony, standing to one side. 'They're saying she's alive.'

Tony shrugs. 'Wait and see,' he says, ever the experienced policeman. 'They might not be talking about the same person.'

'They are! They just recognised her from the photo.'

'Well, let's just see. Take it as it comes.'

Tony's professional scepticism is all very well, but looking at the happily smiling faces of these women, I know what I think. All that weirdness of Bobby wanting to come and then not wanting to come has an explanation. My sister isn't dead. For reasons of their own, Bobby and my aunt were lying to me. She's here, just across the fields.

Now a woman in a brown *salwar kameez* and a grey headscarf is leading us off down the street. The other women gather round us as we follow. We pass in a troupe through the arch and out into the open countryside. Anup runs over to Inder in the car and explains what's happening.

We follow the women down a narrow tarmac lane for a hundred yards or so. Then there's a dirt track off to the right, a big expanse of ripe, waving corn to the left, the bare grey earth of a newly harvested field to the right. The women march on, purposefully.

My head is spinning. I had such an odd feeling about yesterday. As we sat in the bar last night I even said to Anup, 'I'm not really going to believe Bachanu is dead until somebody from her family tells me she is.' And the truth was, I didn't really feel anything about her being dead, apart from a burning sense of injustice that my siblings hadn't told me. It was difficult to mourn a sister I had never known.

As we walk on, past a sprawling haystack and a red tractor, and turn left at the corner of the field, new worries flood in. OK, so my sister is alive, but what if one of my family is there with her? I can see the farm now, up in a clump of trees at the end of the track: two low yellow buildings on the left, a few cows by a concrete water butt on the right. There's a blue trailer parked next to two oil drums. What if I get to the end of this track and find Ginda is visiting? Or Prakash? My stomach is suddenly wobbly with butterflies.

Tony is still being the sceptical policeman. 'Let's not

jump to any conclusions,' he's saying, 'until we see how this all unfolds and unfurls.'

What if Bobby was lying to us so he had time to warn my sister? Or what if he was protecting me and Bachanu won't see me after all? Yesterday evening I finally stopped worrying about my worst fear: being rejected by my sister. Now I'm straight back in that dark and frightening place again.

I stop in the middle of the track. 'Sunny,' I say, 'I'm not sure I can go in there now.'

'Why?'

'What if somebody from my family is there?'

'Don't be silly. Why would they be here?'

'They might be. I know they come here. It's the time of year my mother used to come. They might be here on a visit. I couldn't face it.'

'Sunny,' says Tony. 'Why don't you go ahead? Find out what the crack is. We'll wait here.'

So Anup turns and walks on behind the gaggle of women, a confident figure in his shiny crimson 'Fly Emirates' T-shirt and fitted white shorts that stop just below his knees.

'Why don't you have a sit on that log, Jasvinder?' says Tony. But I prefer to remain standing. I'm literally shaking as I watch the colourful little figures of the village women walk past the water butt and the cows and on into the farmyard. Other people appear, surrounding them. To the right I can see a man in a big white turban. 'I think that's Gurdial,' I say to Tony. He looks like the Gurdial in the photograph, who also wears a big white turban.

Then Anup has turned and is waving at us.

'He's beckoning,' says Tony.

He is, his right hand cupped. Later, he tells me that my sister asked, 'Is it Susie?', just as my aunt did yesterday.

'You've got no problems here,' Tony is saying.

I start to move forward. Slowly, feeling every step, my legs like lead. Can this be happening, can it be true, that my sister really is alive? Then coming out from one side of this little crowd I see a tiny white figure, beetling determinedly past the trailer and the oil drums, turning onto the track.

'Is it her?' I say. As she gets closer my heart turns over. I see the nut-brown face, the prominent teeth I recognise from the photographs I've kept for all these years. 'It is. It *is* her,' I mutter.

And here she is! My sister, Bachanu, alive and well and coming straight at me. She's all in white: her off-white *salwar kameez* is almost totally covered by the long white shawl that is wrapped tightly round her head, which flows down over her shoulders and back. As her arms come up she breaks into a run.

I stand frozen on the track. Are my legs moving? Am I here? Is it her? Can this be really happening at last? We fall into an embrace. My head is over her shoulder, staring at a few broken brown leaves on the dry dirt of the track. I break into sobs. *Oh my God, it is her, and I am here with my sister at last.*

'Why are you crying?' she says, her hand patting my back as she clasps me in a tight embrace.

'They said you were dead.'

'Who said that to you?'

'My aunt Jagji and Bobby. Yesterday. We saw them in Kang Sabhu.'

'Don't cry. I'm here, *putt*. I'm your sister and I'm here.'

I hold her tight. I want to make sure I've got her, that it is her, and she's real.

Eventually she unclasps herself. She turns to greet Tony, who is standing to one side.

'*Sat sri akal.*'

'*Sat sri akal*,' he says, word perfect. He has the hugest grin on his face.

'Come along,' says Bachanu, to me, in Punjabi. She puts a hand round my waist. The push she gives me is the same as my aunt gave me, yesterday, in Kang Sabhu: hard, forceful, no-nonsense, the push of the Punjabi *bibi*. Then I am into the farmyard, past the five village ladies who led us here, who are standing staring at me, unsmiling, like some sort of tableau; on past another group of women seated on low chairs and *manja*, looking up, bright-eyed at this new arrival. I notice a big semicircular pile of vivid orange sweetcorn on the swept dirt of the yard. Then we're on through a shady veranda and into a darkened room. Bachanu shows me to a sofa covered with a shiny salmon-pink quilt, next to a television in a polished wood cabinet, with shelves and drawers below and a mirror above. She throws open some shutters and light floods in through a window.

Now I am being introduced to other family members. Another old woman in a white scarf and long, white *salwar kameez*; then a tall jolly man with a bushy pepper-and-salt beard and a high, loose turban: he is Bachanu's oldest son. Then another son, Parminder, and two daughters-in-law, who embrace me with warm hugs. Then Gurdial himself is in the room. I was right – he was the man in the big white turban. Beneath his fine headgear he is a quiet, handsome man with a little grey moustache and smooth skin the colour of teak. He doesn't look much older than his bearded son. He shakes my hand with a gentle nod, then retreats to an armchair in the corner. He is a pussy-cat, not the scary figure of my imagination. I sit next to Bachanu on the sofa. Her son sits next to her on the other side and the other old woman next to Anup on the single bed oppo-site. I have no idea who she is. Gurdial's sister perhaps. I bring out my photographs. The picture of Bachanu with the tractor, the picture of Gurdial in his turban, the tiny picture of Dad as a young man, on the back of which is stamped 'May 1958'.

Bachanu turns it over in her hand. 'I recognised you straightaway outside,' she says. 'Because you have your father's features.'

'This must have been taken when he first went over to England,' I say. 'Maybe for a passport.'

'He went over twice,' says Bachanu. 'In between he came back to marry me to Gurdial.'

'So that's why he came back.'

'He stayed two years. Then he took your mother away with him. With the children.'

'But not you?'

Bachanu smiles. Even though she's old and her face has deep wrinkles, it's a bright, effervescent, toothy grin, like

Anna and Jordan.

the excited grin of a child. 'I was married. So they didn't need to take me.'

Now I bring out the photograph of Natasha and Anup. 'This is my daughter Natasha,' I tell her. 'With Anup here. They are to be married next year. He is my . . . what's son-in-law, Sunny?'

'*Jawai*,' he says.

'He is my future *jawai*.'

Bachanu smiles as Anup grins from the bed opposite. 'Another Sunny,' says Bachanu.

'Another Sunny.'

Then I show her pictures of Anna and Jordan. 'They are lovely children,' she says.

'Thank you. But I don't have as big a family as you.'

She laughs. 'So you saw Jagji and Bobby yesterday? In Kang Sabhu?'

'Yes. They told me you were dead.'

'That was wrong of them.' She smiles. 'Look at me, I'm very much alive.'

'I wasn't going to believe them, until I heard it from Gurdial. That's why I wanted to come here today.'

'I'm so pleased you did, because you could have turned back.'

'I've come a long way for this,' I say. I would never have gone to Kang Sabhu at all, I tell her, if I had known she was here. 'I only went there because I thought that's where you lived. All the letters Dad used to get when we were children, they all came from Kang Sabhu.'

It's strange, I think, even as I say this, that I've had Kang Sabhu so firmly in my head; I know perfectly well that girls always leave home when they get married. Bachanu shrugs. She knows why Jagji and Bobby lied to me, she goes on: because there was a family dispute after my father died.

'I phoned your sisters in England about it at the time, but they didn't want to do anything about it. Didn't they tell you?'

'I don't talk to them.'

'Why not?' Her question is asked with clear eyes and it suddenly dawns on me that she knows nothing about my disownment. They haven't told her – none of them, not even my father. Just as Yasmin and Robina's stories were edited for foreign consumption, so has mine been. I look over at Anup and Tony, sitting side by side on the bed opposite with their glasses of Coke. 'She's asking why my sisters don't talk to me,' I say in English. 'Shall I tell her the truth now?'

'Your call,' says Tony.

Anup shrugs.

'So what do they say to you about me?' I ask.

'They always say you live far away from them. So they don't see you and they don't know what's happening with you. But I always wondered. Why you didn't speak to them on the phone.'

Far away from them! Apart from Prakash, we all lived in Derby. At one time I lived right round the corner from Ginda.

It is time to tell my sister the truth. God help me, maybe she will still reject me, maybe this beautiful welcome will turn sour even at this late stage. But I can't not tell her what has really happened. I have come so far. And I always said, didn't I, that Bachanu must accept me for what I am. Bobby and Jagji accepted me, even though they lied to me. Surely their acceptance of me wasn't another part of their falseness? Surely they were sincere about that, at least?

'My sisters don't talk to me,' I say, 'and it all began when I ran away from home when I was fifteen. My mother showed me a photograph of the man I was supposed to marry, but I couldn't go through with it. I told them I wanted to stay on at school and finish my education, but they wouldn't listen. They took me out of school and kept me at home until I would agree to the marriage. Mum said that it was written that I should get married to this man, that if I didn't it would be the whole family's *bezti*, our shame. So in the end I ran away from home.'

As I tell her the story, Bachanu sits beside me, bright-eyed, shifting her position from time to time, pulling her left leg up onto the bed, putting it back down again, more like a restless child than an old lady. She has the same blue flip-flop sandals that all the *bibis* in Kang Sabhu were wearing. They're quite a contrast to her wrinkled old feet.

She knows the name of the man I should have married, though not that I had refused him. She knows that he married Lucy, but not that that was as a replacement for me.

'I rang Mum,' I tell her, 'and I told her that I wanted to come home, which I did, but that I wouldn't marry that man. She told me that in their eyes I was dead. I had dishonoured their family and I was disowned. Since then, for twenty-nine years, I've been on my own. My sisters don't speak to me . . .'

I tell her how I brought my three children up by myself and never asked my family for anything, how all I ever wanted was their affection and approval, how I had secret relationships with some of my sisters, but it was always difficult, because the public image of them not talking to me always had to be maintained. How I asked my father once whether I could come to India with him and he refused – he told me that I would bring my shame with me.

When I have finished I look up at her. She says nothing, just reaches out with one of her strong, bony, wrinkled hands and places it on mine. It is clear from her silence and the warmth in her bright eyes that she has accepted everything I've told her.

'For twenty-nine years,' she says, 'you have been sitting in England thinking you couldn't come here. When as far as I'm concerned you could have come here whenever you wanted.'

'So you don't think I've shamed you? Dishonoured you?'

'Not at all. This wasn't your fault. There was no need for your mother to say that to you. She should have known better. The trouble is, your father would have sat there and he wouldn't have said a thing.'

'That's how Dad was,' I say.

'Yes, we both know how he was.'

She slaps me on the back and lets out a loud bark of a laugh. With that, she gets to her feet. I follow her outside. In the shade of the veranda are three *manjas*, arranged in a loose oblong, a place to sit and chat in the gentle sunshine of an Indian winter's day. To me, Bachanu gestures to the one in the middle, which has a green plastic cover over criss-crossed green plastic twine. Then she turns. 'You must see our tractor,' she says to Anup and Tony. 'The boys will show you.'

So Anup and Tony go off to look around the farm with Bachanu's teenaged grandchildren and I sit with my sister on the *manja*.

Now that we are alone together she tells me that my mother had never been very kind to her either. 'When my mother died and your mother married my father she didn't want me to live with them, so I was sent to live with my grandmother. Her mother. She brought me up.'

'How old were you then?'

'I was only nine months old. My mother had TB.'

'My father always told us she was bitten by a snake and died in a rice field.'

'No. She died from TB. She was always ill, a very poorly woman.'

Some time after Dad married my mother, he went to England for five years. Then he came back for two years and organised Bachanu's wedding. But before he arranged for her to be married he and my mother argued about her. Dad wanted to take her to England with them and Mum refused. She said, 'If she goes to England then I'm not going to England.' To which Dad replied, 'From this day forward I will never sit down and eat *roti* with you.'

'You're right,' I say, thinking back to how they were when I was a child. 'If I look back I can never remember them eating together.'

'You see! You know how things were, just like me.' Once again my sister slaps me on the back and laughs.

That may explain a lot. When I came in from school it was me that used to make Dad his breakfast and sit and eat with him before he went off to work the night shift. He and Mum never sat down to a meal together. All the time we lived in Dale Street while I was growing up they slept in separate rooms. You never saw them being affectionate together. Their marriage was almost like a business relationship. Mum could be quite bossy with him, too. She wouldn't allow him to smoke in the house and if people were coming round she'd tell him to dress in a certain way. I think that's probably why he talked to himself so much.

'But Mum came to see you when she was out here?' I say. We were always told she did; that was why she took our old clothes and cast-offs. I can still hear her voice, 'Bachanu needs these things. She is very poor. We have to help her.' She always said she took money towards the tractor, too.

'She used to come here to marry her daughters off,' my sister replies. 'After they were married she would show her face here for a day or two. Show people she was from England. Then she would go off and stay at the in-laws' house. She wouldn't stay here.'

'But she did used to help you. Bring you bits and pieces from home?'

'She did help us. But I don't think it was out of love. It was more out of duty. Or guilt even. She was a *bewkoof*.'

I laugh at that, because it comes out of nowhere and it's clearly not meant out of malice. *Bewkoof* means an idiot – or a fool. I can imagine my mother here, very much as my sister has described, the female version of the peacock, striding in, showing off, loving the status of it all. She did this in England, when she was out to impress our other aunties or the community leader. If one of my sisters was about to be married, or a husband had just come over from India, she would parade them around, show off the beautiful clothes, without thinking about what her daughters really wanted, how they might be feeling. Now that I've seen what it's like out here, how people have such regard for England, the prosperity and the status the country represents, I can see it so clearly. Mum would have turned up at this farm for a night or two, bigged it up in front of Bachanu, the niece she had refused to take to England, and left, off to one of the in-laws': Ginda's or Yasmin's, Robina's or Lucy's.

'So what did Mum tell you about us?' If Bachanu hadn't heard about my disownment, what else didn't she know? 'You knew that Robina died?'

'Yes. We were very sad to hear that. They didn't say anything to us about it for a while.' She pauses. 'When your mother finally came out and told me, I asked her why nobody had phoned us earlier. She said, "It's not the kind of thing you say, is it?"' Bachanu raises her eyebrows; she doesn't need to add anything to that for me to get her meaning. 'Then Papa talked to me about Robina when he was here. He was very sad about it all. He said her death was your mother's fault. She could have stopped it.'

I sigh, deeply, thinking again of the meetings I had with Robina shortly before she died, in her house in Leicester, with the dents in the living room walls. She had phoned my mother and been told she had a love marriage, she had made her bed and must now lie in it. Lovely dutiful daughter that she was, she was too impressed by my parents' stupid frozen values to realise that the shame she thought she would cause them was just a figment of their distorted imagination.

'He was probably right,' I say. 'She probably could have stopped it. If she'd been more supportive. But she never took her daughters' side in their marriages, ever.'

There is silence. 'But you know that Pashie's first husband died?' I say.

'Yes. Pashie brought Gurmal over here, so we realised that then.'

'So did you know that Yasmin's husband also died?'

'Yes. And she has married again and had more children.'

So Bachanu knows more than Bobby and my auntie did. I'm surprised my father didn't tell them about me too.

'Did you miss my father?' I ask.

Bachanu's face falls and suddenly she looks so sad. 'I got on with it,' she says. 'Because you have to.'

'And how was it when he came to visit?'

'It was good to see him. He hadn't changed.' She pauses. 'He was here with Robina's son, Sunny. He was full of fun.'

'Yes,' I say. 'Sunny must have been about ten or eleven then.'

'Something like that.'

'You know,' I say, 'that was the time I wanted to come. I asked Dad if I could come, but he wouldn't let me.'

'No? But he spoke about you a lot. He said that you were the one that took the best care of him. Before you went to work you'd pop into the house and see how he was. He said you had done very well in England – you were a doctor.'

I smile and shrug. I may have got my degree, and even my honorary degree, but I was never a doctor.

'I remember he said you organised funds from the Government for him.'

I realise she means benefits, his pension and so on. I did do that, in his final years. He needed help to fill in the forms.

'And vitamins,' she says. At first she gets the word wrong and I don't hear it properly. 'Vitamins,' she repeats.

'Oh, vitamins.' Yes, I remember I was trying to get him to take vitamin tablets at the time.

All this is a revelation to me. That my father said these things about me out here. But never told them I'd been disowned. I realise now that he was proud of me, even if he never told me that. Perhaps he struggled to express it to me in words because of his fear of what my brother and sisters would think if they knew he was proud of a daughter who had run away from home? So he said all the nice things about me out here instead.

We sit there in silence for a few moments. I'm looking round the farmyard and thinking how idyllic it is here. Simple, of course – there are few luxuries – but my sister has everything she needs. This is the Asian family as it should be. The grandmother, still living at the centre of the family, accorded respect by her children and grand-children. The idea that she is somehow the poor relation, as my mother always tried to make her out to be, is ridiculous.

I say, 'My daughter Natasha is getting married the year after next. I worry because I don't know anything about weddings and I haven't got anything to pass on to her.'

'What do you mean?' my sister asks.

'Of course I went to weddings when I was a child, but I haven't been to any since I ran away. I don't understand the traditions. They're the things your mother teaches you, which I was never taught.'

'I'll come to the wedding, if you like. Show you what to do.'

'Will you?'

'Invite me and I'll be there.'

One of Bachanu's grandsons is standing near to us. His name is Davinder and he must be about twelve. He has lovely clear brown eyes and a mischievous smile. 'Invite me and I'll be there,' she repeats, patting my arm. 'Now I must organise something for you all to eat. Maybe Davinder could show you round the farm.'

I take the hint and get to my feet. Bachanu bustles off towards the centre of the dirt yard, where there's a cooking area at the back of a brick stable. One of the daughters-in-law is already in there, bent over a stove, making chapattis. Just outside, Bachanu's oldest son is kneeling in front of an open fire: three long bits of old, dry wood propped up on a clay cooking area, flames licking around one end. Next to him he has a green plastic bucket full of fresh chicken.

Davinder leads me on, past a washing line where shawls and saris and Westernised men's clothes are hanging out to dry. At the far end of the yard, past an old-fashioned threshing machine, three or four buffalos lie flat out, sleeping in the shade of a spreading tree, tied up by their noses to its trunk. They stir lazily as we pass. Beyond them is a long low building, with two or three dark bedrooms visible and a toilet. So after all, Bachanu and her family did not need to use the fields for their ablutions, as my family had it. On the far side of that the ground slopes down to a field of sugar cane.

'Don't go in there,' Davinder says. 'There are over two hundred snakes. One does this.' He bends up his forearm rapidly like a cobra striking.

'A cobra! You've seen one in there?'

'Yes, I have. The snakes look after the sugar cane and make sure nobody comes to steal it.'

When we get back to the veranda a group has gathered on the *manjas*. Bachanu's eldest son, his wife, one of the other sons, Anup, Tony. Another daughter-in-law is handing round a plate of chapattis and vegetable samosas. Little Davinder sits on his grandmother's knee. Tony is trying out his Punjabi on one of Bachanu's teenaged grandsons and making everyone laugh.

'Bachanu is going to come over for Anup and Natasha's wedding,' I tell them.

'Not just me,' she says. 'I'm going to bring everybody.' She waves round at her husband, her two sons, her daughter-in-law, her four grandsons.

'Everybody!' I say. 'Sunny, are you ready for this?'

They laugh and I translate for Tony. 'Bachanu says she's going to bring the whole family over for Natasha's wedding.'

One of the daughters-in-law has brought a dish of cooked chicken pieces. Now Gurdial has brought out the *desi* and is offering it to Anup and Tony.

'Dad used to make that,' I say. 'In the shed in the garden at home. I caught him once when I was a little girl. With a bunch of his mates, making *desi*.'

Gurdial nods and offers the bottle in my direction.

'Thank you, I'm fine.' I'm excited enough as it is; I'll stick to Coke. 'So what will you say to Ginda when she comes here next year?' I ask my sister.

'I'm going to tell her you've been here.'

'And what if she stops talking to you?'

'*Pher ki hoia*!' So what! I'll just tell her Susie has been here and she's going to come again and bring her children. If she stops talking to me she stops talking to me.'

'So your sisters don't talk to you?' says the oldest son, the jolly bearded man in the patterned turban.

'No, they don't.'

'Does anybody from the family talk to you?'

'Only Gugsy, my nephew. Pashie's son. Pashie disowned him.'

'Why?'

'Because he married out of choice. The last straw for her was he married a *chamar*.'

I wonder how this will go down, but Bachanu is smiling. 'Bring him with you next year,' she says.

Once again I am thrown back to the truth: that for my family over here the things we've done in England, the arrangements we've made about marriages and even divorces are of no concern to them. As Mr Malhotra said to me back in Delhi: Whose honour were your family trying to preserve?

With the food and the *desi* we settle into a relaxed and happy state. I tell them a little bit about our trip out here. How when we went to the Red Fort in Delhi, Tony had a proposal of marriage. How Anup joined us from Amritsar, and that's where we're going to next, to see the Golden Temple. There is more banter about how the whole family is going to come to England for Natasha's wedding. 'Maybe you should charter an aeroplane and park it on our land so you can take us all,' Bachanu jokes.

After we've finished eating, the teenagers get to their feet and take the plates and dishes away to the kitchen area in the middle of the yard. None of the adults have to ask them to do this, and I think of the contrast to teenagers at home, who always need to be told. Here, the young people understand that, as the Punjabis say, a guest is a blessing from God.

The sun sinks lower in the sky and soon it will be time to go. I have already decided that I'm coming back here next year, bringing my children with me. Now that Bachanu has accepted me, I want her to meet them too. 'You say you haven't got a family in England,' Bachanu says at one point, 'you have a family here now.'

She means it, too. After the meal is over, she and I go for a last walk together around the farmstead. She shows me a lemon tree in one corner, then for a few moments we stand on the edge of her little domain, looking out over the field of sugar cane and the flat landscape beyond.

'I'm sorry we didn't bring anything with us,' I say. 'A present for the children or anything. I didn't know what we'd find.'

'Don't say that. What you've given us today far outweighs any material goods you could have brought. Whatever happens, brothers and sisters need to have a bond. That's far more important than anything else.'

As we walk back towards the family group under the veranda, she stops by a *manja* that is under one of her trees, with a nice view out over the sugar cane field and the land beyond.

'Papa sat there on his last visit,' she says. 'He'd sit out

here till the early hours. I'd keep calling him into bed, but he loved it out here. "Oh no, I'm fine," he'd say.' She grins. 'That was the man he was. Happiest with a *desi* under the stars.' She must have missed him so much over the years, but that whole subject feels too big to ask her about now.

As the sun is setting, big and orange over the flat fertile plain, we say goodbye. There are long hugs all round and then we get into the car and drive off. Inder has skilfully managed to find his way down the track and is parked up just outside, by the blue trailer that reads 'Blow horn'.

'What are you going to do about Bobby?' Anup asks, as we bump off towards the main road. 'We said we'd call in on him and your aunt on the way back.'

'Let's leave it,' I say. 'He lied to us and he knows he lied to us. I don't want to see him.'

Tony is all for calling in to Kang Sabhu, having a word with him, and sorting it out; but I don't need that kind of confrontation, not today. I found my sister in the end, that's what matters. Not going back there sends a message in itself. Not just for him, but for my sisters too.

The darkness has already come down as we pass through Kang Sabhu. The lit-up shop signs flash by in under half a minute.

Sitting back in my seat I can hardly believe the day we've had. Was it for real? I text Natasha in England to tell her that Bachanu isn't dead after all, we've found her and she's alive. *Wow, Mum, that is so wonderful,* she texts back. I text her back to tell her she will meet

Bachanu; that I'm going to bring all three children out here next year; that Bachanu has agreed to come over for her wedding.

She sends me a long, loving text back, part of which reads, *I am so glad this trip has brought this, Mum. I am so proud of our Punjabi roots and know we wouldn't be so privileged if it wasn't for our grandparents. I want you to be at the centre of my wedding. People don't get more important than the mother of the bride. Let's embrace our heritage together as a family. That makes it more special.*

Natasha has taken on all the wonderful cultural things about India far more than I have, the clothes, the language, the music, the food. In the past she's kept it all away from me because she didn't want to hurt me. She even used to turn her Asian music off in her car when I got in. She won't need to do that any more. My detachment has been about my pain, but now it's time to start putting past rejections to bed.

When I was with Anup's mum Neelam in Leeds, trying on her Asian suits in her bedroom, she said to me, 'When Natasha gets married we are going to go to India and choose our wedding suits and the dress that Natasha is going to wear.' At the time I thought, 'Yeah, right, as if.' Whereas now I'm not only ready to do that, I am *going* to do that. I'm looking forward to it. What a difference!

Back at the hotel, I text some other people too. My two other children, obviously, and Ranjit – Gugsy – who has been following my trip on a daily basis. There's another man I want to know about this too, as he has become so closely involved in my life, my campaigns and the ongoing struggle of Karma Nirvana.

He contacted me two or three years ago, when the charity was in trouble and there was a real risk that without further funding we would have to close the helpline down. I had pleaded with the then Labour Government, I had put a petition with three thousand signatures on the Number Ten Downing Street website, I had exhausted every avenue. I was desperate. It had got to the point where the helpline capacity was half of what it should be and we had to stop manning it completely in the evenings and at weekends.

We had somehow got our plight onto the news and this man saw it. He contacted Karma Nirvana and said he would like to know more about what we do, to help possibly, but that he wanted to remain anonymous. I was initially sceptical. I thought, 'Yeah, how many times have I heard this before? And it's come to nothing.'

Anyway, nothing ventured, nothing gained. One of my colleagues had an in-depth conversation with him and explained in more detail what we do and what we needed. When she came to me afterwards she told me that he had asked a number of searching questions. 'If I am going to give to your organisation,' he had said, 'I need to know that the money won't be going to line the Chief Executive's or anybody else's pockets.' My colleague could hardly bring herself to tell me this. 'I hope you're not offended,' she said. 'Absolutely I'm not,' I replied. 'That is such a valid question to ask.' I've worked around enough charities and seen how they operate to know that. Naming no names, I've been involved with one where this was exactly what was happening.

So after that, a meeting was arranged. I got together a couple of key colleagues from our team and also some survivors. I wanted this interested party to hear some testimonies, so he could see for himself the importance of the work we do.

We were all gathered in the conference room at the back of Karma Nirvana when in walked . . . a tall, impeccably dressed, Asian man. As he took his seat, I couldn't help but feel challenged. 'Is this man safe?' was my first thought. Perhaps he's come to check us out for some dubious reason of his own. Can he really be on our side?

But as he started to ask questions, and listen to our answers, it soon emerged that he was calm, considerate, full of empathy, and genuinely wanted to hear what we had to say. I immediately felt comfortable with him. I felt I could be completely honest about the fact that we were operating on a shoestring and we might not yet have the greatest procedures in the world. He listened as I explained how we'd had to close the evening and weekend helplines, which we hated to do, as these are the times when often they are needed most.

Then I said, 'I know that when you spoke to my colleague here you asked a question about how you could verify that you wouldn't be giving to a charity where people were lining their pockets. I wholeheartedly appreciate that question. I want you to know that I've worked for Karma

Nirvana as a volunteer for five years now and I've not had a penny from it.'

Then he listened to Shazia and Preet, two survivors of forced marriage whose heartrending stories I have told in *Daughters of Shame*. You could see him welling up despite himself and, watching him, for me that was an indication of sincerity.

At the end of the meeting he stood up and thanked us all. Then he took me aside and wrote me a cheque, right there and then, for five thousand pounds. That was enough to keep the helpline going for three months. I couldn't believe it.

On the one hand I felt *gareeb*, which in Punjabi means 'poor', with an extra sense of feeling proud, not wanting to accept handouts. But on the other hand I felt it was OK to take this man's donation, because he didn't come across as someone who was throwing his money around. I felt he had been humbled by the survivors' stories and his desire to help was genuine.

I pray every day, morning and night, and Karma Nirvana was right at the front of my prayers at that time. I had been asking God to help somehow to keep the helpline going, and here, it seemed, was an answer to my prayer. It felt as if this man had been sent. I thought, 'God up there, you are always challenging me, always leading me forwards. Now you send me an angel in the form of an Asian man. That I could never have imagined, and it fills me with such hope.'

As it turned out, the cheque was just the start of it. Our anonymous supporter didn't just want to give us money, he wanted to help take the charity forward effectively over the next few years. To be honest, as the helpline had been cut back, I had struggled with the whole idea of Karma Nirvana's future. I had felt that everything was against us and maybe the time had come to pack the whole project in. We were banging and banging on doors and nobody was opening them. Why did I need to give myself this ongoing grief? Hadn't I done my bit, wasn't it time now to take a back seat and give myself back a quiet life? But this man's intervention gave me the shot in the arm I needed, that we all needed. As well as money, he has provided two professional fundraisers to work with us. He has started to show us how we can find financial support from other sources; he has put us back on our feet.

That evening, Tony, Anup and I have a celebratory curry and fall into bed, exhausted. 'There are more red herrings in this story than in a tin of John West,' Tony says with a laugh. 'You just couldn't make it up, could you?'

You couldn't either. Just this morning, if the truth be told, I was feeling empty and sad that my trip to Kang Sabhu had ended the way it had. I was trying to feel the same warmth towards my new relatives that I'd longed to feel towards my sister. Having come all this way, somehow to turn them into replacements for this person whose love I craved. But I couldn't fake it. And now . . .

I have found my sister, after all. And what a sister she

is! She turns out to be exactly as I might have imagined her – better than that, with her effervescent spirit, her irreverence and her wild laugh. Off and on we spent the whole day talking. I've learned so much. All the questions I wanted to ask are more than answered. More important than that, I feel we've hit it off, we understand each other, this is a relationship I can really build on. When I get home I shall write to her, tell her more, ask her more. Then next year I'm going to bring my children out to meet her. It really has been a dream come true.

11

Ik-oan-kaar, ik-oan-kaar, ik-oan-kaar . . . . It is 7.30 a.m. and I am standing outside the Golden Temple at Amritsar, my ears filled with an amplified version of the prayer my mother listened to every morning back at home. 'God is one,' it means. *God-is-one, God-is-one, God-is-one.* The chant takes me straight back to my childhood in Derby, lying in bed with a pillow over my head trying to drown out this very same noise; but now, here, outside this grand white stucco front gate to the temple, onion-shaped domes above and tall arches below, I feel I am simultaneously being transported forward into the magical world my mother must have dreamed about when she knelt in our front room listening to this music.

'It's like Mecca for Sikhs,' says Anup, with a chuckle.

Right in front of me, to each side of the main entrance arch, stand two tall Sikh warriors in yellow turbans and blue tunics, which are like wraparound coats with skirts that stop just below the knee, held in at the waist by a wide

Me visiting the Golden Temple.

yellow cummerbund with gold studs. Below that they wear white leggings to the ankle. Their feet are bare. In their right hands they hold long spears, with silver banding around their wooden shafts and narrow triangular heads in gleaming silver. A neatly painted sign above the guard on the left reads, in English and Punjabi, 'Please take wheelchair for handicapped persons from Parkarma Room No 52' and above the guard on the right, 'Please keep your shoes in shoe store'.

We have done just that, exchanging our footwear for a numbered metal token at a shed-like wooden building thirty yards away across the gleaming wet marble tiles. To enter the temple your head must be covered, so Tony and Anup have bought bright orange headscarves from one of the numerous hovering hawkers. My head is already well wrapped with one of Neelam's shawls, today a dark blue one with a colourful floral border. Below that I'm wearing one of her nicest saris, in a pale creamy yellow-orange, with tiny white dots and a floral motif in orange and yellow.

Right in front of the two tall guards is a shallow marble trough, fifteen feet long and eight feet wide, in which pilgrims wash their feet before entering the temple. Here they squat, or bow, or make the hands-together *namaste* gesture, the bright early morning sun casting long blue shadows away across the marble floor, which is a vanishing perspective of white hexagons and grey and brown lozenges and triangles.

Tony, Anup and I step into the water in turn, then out the other side onto black rubber matting and a long strip of porous green material that further dries our feet before we mount three cool marble steps onto a broad green carpet that leads us on down through the central arch to the interior courtyard beyond. This is the entrance my mother would have walked through, every year on her visit to Amritsar. How much it must have meant to her in her great faith, to be here at the centre of it all!

As I reach the end of the arch, I pause at the top of the flight of steps and gasp. Before and below me is the Golden Temple proper, the Harmandir Sahib, marooned at the centre of a vast, still, blue-green pool. Just above the water, the base of the temple is white marble, while its upper two thirds and the towers and upturned lotus-flower domes that adorn its roof are entirely covered in gold. The morning sun shines brilliantly on its eastern end and picks out the long row of cupolas that serve as its battlements. The whole fairytale fantasy is ripplingly reflected in the waters below.

The Golden Temple.

With the other pilgrims I walk slowly down the steps until I reach the Parkarma, the broad marble pathway around the pool. Here I find myself kneeling to pray, the sound of chanting ringing in my ears. *Ik-oan-kaar, ik-oan-kaar, ik-oan-kaar*. I am no longer a Sikh, my disownment put paid to that. I am a Christian now, but I can still pray to the one God, thankful for being here, thankful for having arrived, by His grace.

When I get to my feet after five minutes, I walk to the water's edge and stand looking over towards the magical temple. A long double queue of pilgrims has already formed, shuffling slowly along the narrow causeway that joins the temple to the Parkarma. Their colourful turbans and saris stand out against the white buildings of the encircling court-yard, the *bungas* as they are called, floors and floors of rooms for visiting holy men and others to stay or study.

The Indian name for this enclosed water is Sarovar or Amritsar, which means 'pool of ambrosial nectar' (from this the town took its name). Before it was enlarged and structurally contained, in the sixteenth century, during the time of the fourth guru, Ram Dass, this was a peaceful little lake in a forest. That was how Guru Nanak knew it, when he came to meditate here in the late-fifteenth century; and that was how the Buddha knew it, two thousand years before that. Those plastic bottles my mother brought back with her to Derby didn't just hold water, they held sacred ambrosial nectar, a liquid that made a connection with the very founders of Sikhism.

Before I pay my respects to the temple, I have made an appointment to see a senior Sikh, Mr J. Singh, who works here at the temple and, I've been told, has a comprehensive understanding of Sikh scripture. My dissertation for my degree was on 'Women and Sikhism', and my researches for that overturned a lot of what I'd been told about the religion as a child. But now, coming here, I am not going to pass up the chance of hearing what I have read confirmed by someone who is steeped in the Sikh holy book, the Sri Guru Granth Sahib, who understands the tenets of the religion and can answer my questions from a position of faith and knowledge.

Our appointment is for 8.00 a.m. at the foot of these main entrance steps, and at one minute to eight, a suitable candidate approaches. He has a tall turban in pale yellow, square rimless spectacles, and a long beard, which starts out jet black at the moustache and slowly turns grey towards its bushy tip. Below that he wears a pale gold waistcoat over a white *salwar kameez*. He doesn't, I imagine, find us hard to spot: an Asian woman from the UK with a younger Asian man and a shaven-headed white man who towers above all the other pilgrims in the place.

'Jasvinder Sanghera?' he asks.

'Yes,' I say. '*Sat sri akal.*'

He makes the *namaste*. '*Sat sri akal.* I am Mr Jassi Singh.'

I make the *namaste* in return, as do Tony and Anup. 'And this is my colleague Tony Hutchinson and my son-in-law Anup Manota,' I say. But I am thinking, 'Jassi, what a coincidence, that was the name of my first husband, Natasha's father. This trip has been full of odd little coincidences like that.

'Please follow me,' says Mr Jassi Singh.

He leads us on along the white and pale brown marble tiles of the wide Parkarma, the pool on our right, towards what must be the Eastern gate of the temple, in deep cool shadow against the morning sun. Up the steps through this arch there are gardens to the right, filled with pilgrims, walking, standing, sitting, talking, praying on sunny green lawns or under shady trees. To the left, by contrast, is the rattling din of the vast Guru-ka-Langar or communal kitchen, where up to 35,000 pilgrims a day are fed by volunteers. As we follow Mr Singh through this covered area, we see them below us, squatting cross-legged in long rows on strips of thin crimson carpet, eating from shiny metal dishes divided into compartments. The meal these pilgrims receive is simple: chapattis, dal and sweet porridge. Some seem to be eating alone, others in small groups. The whole courtyard rings with the clatter and clang of metal bowls being loaded onto huge metal trolleys, to be carried away and washed up and returned and refilled with food in an endless cycle. The whole operation is remarkable, and certainly dwarfs the little *langar* we used to have at the Dale Road *gurdwara* in Derby, where food was handed out to people who were not hungry, who were eating it more as a part of the ritual of their worship, part of what they were supposed to do.

Behind the huge kitchen and dining area, a red brick alleyway leads back to a hidden courtyard. 'So,' says Mr Singh, turning to me as we enter this place, 'why are you here and what is it you want to know?'

I explain that I'm here, first and foremost, to see the

Golden Temple, a place I have heard about since I was a child, as my mother was a devout Sikh who worshipped at her *gurdwara* every day of her life. But I also want some questions answered, about what exactly the religion says.

'I see,' says Mr Singh. 'Well, I am happy to help you with that.'

In one corner of the courtyard, by a double doorway to an inner room, sits a turbaned guard at a table, surrounded by chairs. Mr Singh gestures for us to sit.

'Would you like tea?' he asks. A tray of *chai* appears, in small glasses, with a plate of delicious Indian sweetmeats.

'So,' says Mr Singh, 'would you like me to answer these questions of yours with your companions here or would you prefer to be alone?'

I look over at Anup and Tony, sipping *chai* and eating sweetmeats, and I suddenly decide I would rather be alone. 'Are you OK if we go and chat privately for a few minutes?' I ask them.

'Whatever you want,' says Tony. 'Sunny and I can chew the fat here.'

'Or rather, the sweetmeats,' says Anup.

'Please follow me,' says Mr Singh. He gestures at a pile of plastic flip-flop sandals near the table. Once we have each found a suitable pair and put them on, he leads me across the little courtyard – which is strewn, I now see, with odd bits of rubbish, a tangle of wire, a slew of loose and broken bricks – and up into a narrow dark staircase on the far side. I follow his bare feet in his flapping sandals up two floors and emerge into the bright sunshine of a flat asphalt roof.

The view from up here is breathtaking: the Golden Temple on its little island, the great square turquoise pool around it, the marble walkway and the white stucco wedding cake buildings surrounding that.

Mr Jassi Singh gestures me to sit then joins me, cross-legged, overlooking the scene. From down below, the amplified chants ring up, bouncing off the buildings, hanging in the air. Just above us, a flock of pigeons dives and flutters, their dark shadows swirling in circles over us and the flat roof.

'Please tell me your questions,' he says.

'I have come from England to the Punjab for the first time in my life. My father and mother were born here and both of them were Sikhs and they brought me and my sisters up as Sikhs in England. When we were little we used to go to *gurdwara*, in the morning Mum would do *paatth*, and would get the holy water and put it on us, and she would tell us all about growing up and being good Sikh girls. But to be honest, all I've ever understood about the Sikh religion is how it oppresses people.'

Mr Singh stops nodding for a moment, but his strong arms remain folded in his lap. 'Why?' he asks.

'From when we were twelve years old my mother used to say to us, "*Likhian*," meaning "It is written", in the Guru Granth Sahib, that you have to marry who we say. She took each of my sisters out of school when they were fifteen and brought them over to the Punjab and forced them to marry. When it came to my turn I said no. I said, "I want to go to college, I want to make something of my life." I said, "Surely, in Sikhism, God wants what's best for us, isn't it enough that I live a good life?" "No," my mother said, "you have to do as I say." So she took me out of school, she kept me at home, and when I was almost sixteen I ran away. I refused to marry the man she wanted me to, so she wouldn't let me come back home. She said, "You've done our shame, our *bezti*. People in the *gurdwara* are talking about us. So you can't come back." So my first question to you is: was that right, in terms of the Sikh religion? Does the Guru Granth Sahib say you must marry who your parents choose?'

The bobbing of Mr Singh's head has turned to vehement shakes. 'No, no, no,' he says. 'Never, never, never.' He unclasps his arms and holds up a single finger. 'That is never written there. Not even in a single stanza, a single paragraph of the Guru Granth Sahib can you find anything like that.'

'So why do people say this, why do they do this?'

'These are illiterate people, they haven't read the Guru Granth Sahib, they haven't followed it properly.'

'So tell me, was I wrong to say no to a forced marriage, when I was fifteen? Have I dishonoured my family?'

'No. This is totally wrong. Because at that time, at that age, a child would not even know what is marriage anyway.'

'OK,' I say, 'my second question relates to caste. When we were little, my mother used to say to us, "You are *jatt*, be proud of that, do not mix with *chamar*, *saini* or any other caste."' I tell Mr Singh the story of going into the *gurdwara* when I was nine, getting slapped by my mother on the head for pointing out that people don't have their caste written on their backs.

Mr Jassi Singh doesn't smile; instead he holds up his finger again and waves it ominously. 'Guru Granth Sahib is for every human being,' he says. 'How to lead your life, what to do with your life. As far as the caste system is concerned, when this temple was founded by our fifth guru, Guru Arjan-Dev-ji, they especially brought a Muslim saint from Lahore to lay the foundation stone. Because Guru-ji wanted to abolish the caste system from the world. So they did that and after that they gave four gates to the temple. Please take a look.'

He stands, suddenly and theatrically, and gestures out towards the temple with the length of his entire arm. 'One, two, three and four. The meaning of these four gates, is that anybody, from any corner of the world, can come to this place of worship, irrespective of caste, creed, colour or anything like that.'

'So might you say these distinctions of caste are man-made?'

'They are man-made, for sure. Any human being is invited here. There is no caste system in the Sikh religion. It never says anywhere in the Guru Granth Sahib that caste is supreme. Guru-ji only is supreme. He is one, he is omnipotent, he is omnipresent, he is everyone's heart and soul, and if you faithfully believe, you can find him.'

'So I wasn't wrong to stand up for what I believed in, either in relation to caste or my marriage?'

'No. You were not wrong. They were wrong.'

'And what would you say to any young men or women who are being told by their parents or anyone else that they have to marry because it's written in the Guru Granth Sahib?'

'I would say . . . these are wrong notions, these are wrong preachings, this is not the Sikh religion.'

I am happy to have that confirmed; this is a message I will definitely be taking home with me.

'My third question has to do with women. My mother always used to say that women didn't have a place in Sikhism.'

Now Mr Jassey Singh looks positively outraged, if not confused. 'Who said that?' he asks.

'My mother used to say that to me.'

His head shakes slowly again. 'No, no, no, no,' he repeats. 'Never, never, never.' He waves his hand at me and explains how women have always been a part of Sikhism. When Guru Nanak first appeared, indeed, it was his sister, Bebey Nanki, who first realised that here was a person who had been directly sent by God. 'That He is the Blessed One. And that one day He will preach the message of Lord God.'

Men have five symbols in Sikhism, he continues, gathering speed: *kesh*, uncut hair, which remains uncut throughout life, because hair is a gift from God; *kanga*, the wooden comb, symbol of cleanliness, used to keep the hair tidy under the turban; *kara*, the iron bracelet, which serves as a reminder for Sikhs to remember their morals; *kachera*, the cotton shorts, which reminds Sikhs to control their bodily lusts and remain chaste; and *kirpan*, the curved dagger, which symbolises the Sikh's responsibility to protect the innocent. But women may adopt these five symbols too. 'So, you see, we have given full respect to the women also.'

'It's sad for me to think,' I say, 'that because of my

experience, I walked away from Sikhism. I thought it was bad. I thought it made my life unhappy. It made me not have any religion for many years.'

Mr Singh is shaking his head again. 'You see,' he says, now with a warm inclusive smile, 'the Sikh religion is a very simple religion. It hugs you, it welcomes you. When you sit and read the Guru Granth Sahib, it is very soothing. Close your eyes and you can feel you are in another world. You feel blessed. If you read the Gurbani daily you will feel blessed.'

I tell him in general terms about the work that I do now, that I am helping young women and men get themselves on the right path, away from what they have been forced to do.

Mr Singh nods at me and smiles. He tells me that through the work I am doing I am in effect a disciple. 'Which is what Sikh means. It means "disciple". You are helping others now, that is your life. And then the next generation will see you, and they too will do good things, because they will follow you.'

I look away from Mr Singh and out over the courtyard. Just below us, across the pool, the queue edges slowly forward across the causeway towards the entrance of the Golden Temple, then little figures emerge from one of the doorways at the side before heading back along the walkway by the water. In the distance, on the far side of the lake, crowds of pilgrims stroll along the Parkarma to the continual music of the chant.

'What you have told me,' I say, 'about the Sikh religion is beautiful. The way it is written is beautiful. So why do some people not follow that, why don't they practise what is written there?'

Mr Singh shrugs. 'Not everyone in the world is a good person. The good and the bad people, the balance is in the hand of God. So we can only pray that whoever reads the Guru Granth Sahib, in whatever corner of the world, they follow that. I pray to God Almighty to bless them all.'

I thank him. I tell him that I'm going to take his message home and use it in the public speaking I do. That the Sikh religion is a beautiful, compassionate religion that has no time for caste, in which women are equal and it is not written anywhere that a woman should force her children to marry.

'Yes,' he says. 'Most definitely, yes.'

'Before I go,' I say, 'are there any specific passages in the Guru Granth Sahib that you can suggest to me, to help empower me with these messages?'

He smiles again. He tells me I must take an English copy of the Guru Granth Sahib away with me from the temple and start reading it. Then I will find stanzas and verses that will back up what he has told me. 'If there is even *one* verse you can find,' he says, waving his finger again, ' to help you in the Guru Granth Sahib, take it and please use it.'

Downstairs, Anup and Tony have finished their *chai* and the plate of sweetmeats and are waiting. I explain that I am going to buy an English copy of the Guru Granth Sahib and then I would like to visit the temple. We follow Mr Singh out and round through the din and clatter of the Guru-ka-Langar, back past the gardens and down the steps to the Parkarma, then on round the walkway and up through the main entrance to the Information Office, where I take possession of the eight volumes of the Holy Book, wrapped in a shiny silver and turquoise cloth, tied at the top with a gold ribbon. Leaving this with one of Mr Singh's colleagues for the morning, we go back inside the temple complex and make our way round to the causeway out to the temple. There are two queues in, and one broader walkway out, separated by golden railings. Every five yards or so, at the top of a marble pillar, is a gilded square lantern, like something out of a Victorian street in London, only topped with an onion dome. As we inch closer to the Harmandir Sahib, the intricacy of the surface of the temple becomes clear. The upper wall of gold is dense with raised patterns: flowers, foliage, fish, animals, even a few human figures parade across its gleaming surface. Below it, the white marble is intricately inlaid with patterns of brightly coloured semi-precious stones (onyx, mother-of-pearl, lapis lazuli, red carnelian, amongst others, I discover later).

After my talk with Mr Singh, I feel both enlightened and empowered. I want to go and bow down before the Guru Granth Sahib. I am a Christian, but Mr Singh has given me permission to worship here in any way I want. Sikhs welcome all comers. For the first time since I was disowned I feel part of all this. I feel I understand the beauty of the Sikh religion and I want to be included in it.

When you walk into a *gurdwara* in England, people always stop and look at you and ask you where you're from. The *bibi*-network is in full force back home. But here I don't feel that. As I stand in the long queue with Anup and Tony, I'm completely anonymous. Nobody knows or cares who I am, nobody is watching me. We are just more pilgrims, queuing here on Guru Nanak's birthday. It feels so real, so unhypocritical, so peaceful. I find myself thinking, 'Mum, I wish you were here with me.' I am itching to bow down where she bowed down, to follow in her footsteps, see what she saw.

As we reach the Harmandir Sahib, we duck through a little side door with the moving queue of pilgrims and find ourselves in the lavishly ornamented interior. In the centre of the floor, behind gold railings, is a huge Guru Granth Sahib, propped up on a red velvet cushion. Two holy men with white tunics and blue turbans sit silently in front of it, high above it is a square crimson canopy, embroidered with gold and hung around its edge with extravagant gold tassels. Behind the velvet cushion are strings of fresh flowers, white and orange and crimson, making a floral oblong on the floor, which further over is strewn with coins, offerings of the passing pilgrims. To one side are more turbaned holy men, sitting cross-legged, chanting into microphones. It is their singing, I realise now, which rings continually round the courtyard complex outside (the *kirtan*, the intoning of devotional prayers). Every inch of the walls and ceiling is covered with gold: swirling in filigree patterns or inlaid with coloured glass and precious stones. There are golden arches above and between golden pillars, there are balconies which exterior light shines in through, from when other turbaned heads look down. From the centre of the golden, jewel-encrusted ceiling hangs a spectacular chandelier.

As I bow down before the Holy Book I feel an

overwhelming sensation of awe. Here I am, in the holiest place in Sikhism, where saints and gurus have worshipped before me over the centuries. I'm not here because my mother or anyone else has brought me, I'm here in my own right. Furthermore, I've just spoken in depth to a Sikh holy man who has verified for me that all the things I always thought were true, are true. I feel vindicated.

At this point I am aware of one of the holy men staring at me. My immediate thought is that he has somehow realised I shouldn't be here, I am not worthy, I am not a true Sikh. He moves towards me. 'Put your headscarf on,' he says, 'put your headscarf on.' In my emotion Neelam's blue scarf has slipped. I pull it back over my head and continue with my prayers to my God, a God entirely welcomed by the Sikh faith.

After I was disowned I was a complete atheist for years. Part of that was to do with a feeling of 'Why me? If there was a God, why would He have let this happen to me?' Part of it was also because I had consciously abandoned Sikhism. As I told Mr Jassi Singh just now, I thought it was an oppressive religion. My mother used it to justify everything she did, as I now know, mistakenly. So I detached myself from it, as survivors often do with the religion they have been brought up with, be it Sikhism, Hinduism, Islam or anything else. I even stopped celebrating Diwali, though I was frequently living in Asian neighbourhoods where it was hard to avoid the lights shining a welcome in every window.

Then in 1996 I got to know a woman called Sharon. I met her through the keep-fit classes I ran. She was a woman of Caribbean background but we had so many things in common. Her sister had died of leukaemia very young, just as I had lost Robina. At a time in my life when I was feeling very low, split from my second husband, Rajvinder, pregnant with Jordan, living in a tiny cold half-finished house in Derby, Sharon used to come and bring me food and cheer me up. We would sit together in the one room that was habitable in that place and after we had eaten, Sharon would pray out loud, for my two children, for the baby that was on the way, for me to have a good life. The first time she did it I was rather wary, but the regular ritual soon started to make me feel a whole lot better. When she'd left I always felt at peace. So I started to be curious about this religion that gave Sharon so much joy and strength, that had calmed me in my darkest hour. I thought, 'I'm going to find out more about this.' Sharon never forced it down my throat. Her attitude always was, 'It works for me. What have you got to lose by finding out about it?' She gave me my first Bible.

Then, at her suggestion, I went on an Alpha course, which is basically a set of open meetings that allows you to ask difficult questions about Christianity, particularly how it works in the modern world. 'If there is a God, how could He have allowed the Holocaust to happen?' You discuss, head-on, the most problematic issues there are. The course is also completely non-prescriptive. It doesn't say that you have to go to church every Sunday and do this or that ritual to be a good Christian. You can worship God anywhere: in your house, or your car, or wherever being close to Him helps you.

So I started to read the Bible, the Book of Psalms especially, to start with. Some of the Psalms are fantastic, because they are basically affirmations. I'd often found affirmations helpful, but never before from a particular religion. Now I was using these verses from the Bible in my daily life. The whole thing just grew and grew. I started to go to a cell group, where you sit in people's houses and discuss Bible passages, interpret them for yourself. That group became like another family for me. I was happy to go. Nobody was telling me to do this. Nobody was brainwashing me. It was me allowing myself to be me.

I started to pray every day. Then in 1998 I got baptised in a church at the top of Normanton Road, the same road I ran up when I ran away from home. I was one of three adults becoming Christians that day. The other two were a mixed-race couple: an Asian man, Ravi, and his white wife, Sylvia. In front of us was a stage that turned into a huge pool of water and one by one we walked up to it, fully dressed, before being guided down steps into it by the priest who prayed over us as we submerged ourselves, head and all. I came up dripping and exultant. 'This is it,' I thought, 'I'm new born.' Sharon and my children were there to witness this, even Jordan, who was just eighteen months old, racing around the church in a cream knitted jumper with his curly hair everywhere.

Since then I've been a Christian, proud to say I walk in faith. I open every day with a prayer, and at the end of every day, I pray. I always end every prayer 'in the armour of God'. Ravi gave me that, right at the start of my believing. He said to me, 'Jasvinder, you've been called to carry other people on your back. So I would suggest you end every prayer "in the armour of God".' My children know it off by heart: we wear the helmet of salvation, the breastplate of righteousness, the belt of truth, the shoes of peace and we carry the sword of the living spirit. Every day.

The other thing that's stayed in my life from those Alpha course days is the use of the word 'Revoke'. As I've gone through life I've had so many bad words used about me, and put onto me, that it got to the point where I started to believe them. 'You will never amount to anything,' my mother said, after I ran away from home. 'You will end up as a prostitute.' And so on. Negative, demoralising things to grind me down and bend me to her will. When she said these things to me back then, I internalised them and believed them all. For years I really did think I was a horrible human being who would never get anywhere in life. But after my baptism I took on the idea of 'Revoke'. If people use bad words against you, or you bring bad words into your life yourself, you can send them back and replace them with good words.

Hate, for example, is a word I don't use and I've taught my children not to use. It is such a strong and negative word. If Anna and Jordan fall out and say, 'I hate you', I say, 'Revoke that! You don't hate your sister. Replace it with a good word.' If one of my children says, 'I'm rubbish' or 'I'll never amount to anything', I say, 'You will, so please revoke that and replace it with, "I will amount to something." It's basically about self-belief. For me, my desire, maybe even my need to do this goes back to those dark days when my parents and family were wishing bad on me all the time. I revoke all that. I replace it with the idea that I am good, that I can do good, that I am doing good. My children use it all the time. Even Anup does now. It's something that rubs off.

Before I speak at any event I slip into the loo and pray before I go on stage. I say, 'Lord, use me as a vessel to speak to these people.' This moment of prayer gives me strength – and sometimes more than that. Shortly before I came out here I was invited to speak in Southall before an audience of Punjabi-speaking Sikh women. It was an event about the Forced Marriage Act and what it meant. I hadn't had the practice I've had since we've been in India, so my Punjabi was very rusty. I speak English with my own children and not having been around my family, I hadn't spoken the language for years. Nobody told me I had to speak Punjabi on that day, but I watched the previous speakers and they weren't engaging this audience at all. Some of the women were literally nodding off. So when I got up I opened my speech in Punjabi. I found the language had returned to me without my trying. Then I did 70 per cent of it in Punjabi. The words flowed out of me. And as for the audience! They sat up and were on the edge of their seats because they could at last understand what was being said.

I was supposed to be leaving no later than 8.00 p.m. to get a train back to Yorkshire. But when the event was over I couldn't get away. There were more illustrious speakers than me there – Lord Lester was one – but these women flocked round me, relaying their stories. I didn't get back home 'til three in the morning. Now, no one would say that was divine intervention, but the point is simply that in situations like that I draw strength from my faith. I feel supported and I do things better.

Up narrow stairs, the first floor of the Harmandir Sahib is altogether airier. Here another huge Holy Book sits at the centre of a bay window, its pages being slowly turned by a man in a white *salwar kameez* and blue turban. He carries a grander version of the same horsehair whisk that I remember from the Dale Road *gurdwara* in childhood, which he waves over the elaborate script of the pages. The walls are covered with huge panels of gold filigree, each with a square mirror at its centre. On the ceiling, between golden arches, is another silken canopy, this one with a pattern of wild crimson roses on a background of pale green. This is a calmer, almost more beautiful space than the big chamber downstairs, and I stand with Anup and Tony for a good two minutes, just drinking in the atmosphere, the sense of peace as the holy man turns the pages, while behind him the lightest breeze comes through the bay windows open to the lake beyond.

The third and top floor, the Shish Mahal, or Mirrored Room, is even simpler. Here, between the tiny mirrors of the walls, there is just a crimson carpet by the holy man turning his pages. From here, you can step out onto a little balcony and look down over the surrounding waters of the Sarovar.

As the three of us descend to the ground floor, a turbaned man follows us, washing the the marble steps behind us as we go. *Seva*! And in the holiest place of all. We make our way back over the causeway, at a faster pace than the slowly shuffling queue going in. By the tall golden gateway at the far end, the Darshana Deorhi, we are given *prashad*, the sweet mixture of sugar, ghee and wheat flour that is a gift from God. We used to get that in Derby too, and I remember as a child that was the one thing I used to look forward to about going to the *gurdwara*. After three hours of agonised cross-legged sitting, you would finally get this sweet pudding at the end.

'Shall I meet you by the holy water place,' I say to Anup and Tony. 'I'd just like to be on my own for a couple of minutes.'

I walk on down along the Parkrama for a few yards and stand looking out over this perfectly serene square lake. Suddenly I am in tears. I am standing sobbing like a child. Why couldn't I have done this with my mother while she was alive? I feel robbed, exactly as I did of my father under that shady tree in Kang Sabhu. Why couldn't Mum have brought me here and taken me into that temple and explained what it all meant to her, why she got up every morning at five and listened to that music – to *this* music, sung by the holy men I've just seen, ringing ethereally round this huge courtyard. Why did my sisters and I have to believe that big lie: that we had to come out here and be married because 'it was written'. It wasn't written. That was all evil nonsense, my mother's twisted interpretation of something pure and good. Just as all that rubbish about caste had nothing to do with the Guru Granth Sahib or the true tenets of this religion that my mother held so dear. And she did hold it so dear, that was the stupid thing. Did she know how far her beliefs had strayed from the truth of what was really written? Was she a hypocrite who used the power of her faith to wilfully oppress her own family? Or was she just a misguided woman who got it wrong, who listened to the wrong people, who was misled by the parochial community she was part of, who were so quick to sit in judgement on her – and me?

One of the tall Sikh guards is approaching me.

'Are you all right?' he asks in Punjabi.

'Yes, yes, I'm fine. Thank you, I'm fine.'

'Nobody has offended you?'

'Nobody has offended me, no.' I say. 'Not here.' With that thought I pull myself together and walk off to find my companions.

There is another queue of pilgrims and at the head of it we are offered silver bowls of holy water. 'Are you sure you want to drink that?' Anup mutters.

'It'll be fine. It's holy water. I'm sure it's clean.'

'I think I'll pass if you don't mind.'

I drink a sip and feel complete. That is what my mother would have done, bless her. Visited the temple, eaten her *prashad*, drunk her holy water then got some plastic bottles to fill up and take home with her too.

Despite all I've said about her, I never stopped loving my mother. I didn't tell anyone this for a long time, but in the early days after I'd run away, particularly when Natasha was little, I used to have imaginary conversations with her, just chat away to her about what I'd been up to in the day, how the baby was getting on, that sort of thing. When I did finally share this with someone, it was one of our survivors, Shazia. I thought she might be embarrassed for me, but she laughed. She had done exactly the same in the refuges where she spent the early days after she ran away from her family. She had wanted her mother to go on loving her too.

I meet up with Anup and Tony, go to the Information Office, and pick up my copy of the Guru Granth Sahib, wrapped in its fine turquoise and silver cloth. Then we head off out of the gate and into Amritsar proper. Close to the temple the old walled city is an interlocking maze of narrow streets, crowded with the usual mad traffic. Amritsar is one of India's key tourist destinations, so Tony is no longer the only white face in the crowd. There are tourists in rickshaws and backpackers on foot, doing their best to blend in, avoiding the gaze of anybody who isn't obviously local. The three of us eat lunch in a place that has bare formica tables, like a canteen, but excellent vegetarian curry. Then we do a little shopping. Tony wants to buy a *kara*, one of the Sikh iron bracelets, Anup wants to get Natasha some earrings, and I have promised Jordan a *dhol*, the same kind of Asian drum that my father used to play as a young man. I asked him what he wanted before we left England and that was his answer. 'Just a *dhol*, Mum. If you get it I can learn how to play it for Natasha's wedding.'

Eventually, in among the little shops selling scarves and sandals and suits and suitcases and framed portraits of Guru Nanak and the other nine gurus in all sizes, we find a place that sells musical instruments.

'I've got a thirteen-year-old boy who wants to learn to play the *dhol*,' I tell the shopkeeper, a tall Sikh in a crimson turban.

He is all smiles. 'That is wonderful,' he says. 'That a boy in England wants to learn to play the *dhol*. Where are you from?'

'I live in the North Country.'

'Is it near Leeds?'

'It is, actually, not far from Leeds.'

'I have family in Leeds.'

We carry the *dhol* back to our hotel and though it's extra luggage we could probably do without, I'm thrilled we have got it. Jordan will learn how to play it for Natasha's wedding. I will meanwhile be reading the Guru Granth Sahib, finding verses to back up what Mr Jassi Singh told me about women being equal and caste and forced marriage being wrong.

Oh unwise one, be not proud of thy caste,
For myriad errors flow out of this pride.
Everyone says, 'There are but four castes'.
But it is from God's Sperm that everyone is born.[3]

The lowliest of the lowly, the lowest of the low-born,
Nanak seeks their company. The friendship of the great is
vain.
For, where the weak are cared for, there doth Thy Mercy
rain.[4]

Everyone is high, none seems low to me;
For God is the only Potter Who has made all Vessels;[5]

---

[3] Guru Granth Sahib, p. 1128 (trans. Gopal Singh, p. 1070)
[4] Ibid, p. 15 (trans, ibid, p. 19)
[5] Ibid, p. 62 (trans, ibid, vol 1, p. 58)

From the woman is our birth, in the woman's womb we are
　　shaped.
To the woman we are engaged; to the woman we are
　　wedded.
The woman is our friend and from the woman is the family.
If one woman dies, we seek another, through women are the
　　bonds in the world.
Why call woman evil who gives birth to kings and all?
From the woman is the woman; without the woman there is
　　none.
Nanak: without the woman is the One True Lord alone.[6]

Later that afternoon, we flag down a *tuk-tuk* outside the
hotel and go back through the narrow lanes of the walled
city to the Golden Temple. It is Guru Nanak's birthday
today, the most important day in the Sikh holy year, and
the pilgrims are flooding in to celebrate. Down the steps on
the wide Parkarma they walk and stroll in a continuous
stream, or squat or sit right by the water's edge, candles lit
beside them. The pool is stiller and darker now, a deep
cobalt blue, perfectly reflecting the golden shimmer of the
Harmandir Sahib. As the chanting gets louder, the beat of
drums is heard, competing with the low chatter of voices
all around. It feels ineffably spiritual and serene.

Dusk falls and ten thousand lights come on, draping the
temple, glinting in the water below. Around the wider courtyard too, the long sloping roofs of the white stucco *bungas*
are strung with bulbs, a myriad of tiny points of light,

---

[6] Ibid, p. 473 (trans, ibid, vol 2, p. 467)

Blackpool meets the Vatican. The candles by the water's edge – two, three, five deep – have merged into one fiery line, marking off this giant square of water. A full moon rises between the two tall watchtowers. Then, suddenly, with a loud bang, there are fireworks, exploding in cascades of brilliant colour in front of us across the starry sky, ashy black debris falling around us, on us, into the pool.

I am swamped with emotion. In my wildest dreams I never imagined my journey would go as well as this: that I would see my father's village, and despite the inevitable modernisation, that it would be, in essence, exactly as he described it to me all those years ago; that I would see the house he grew up in and find relatives I had never heard of; that I would meet his great friend who would tell me in what high esteem he and our family were held; that I would find my sister, that she would accept me, and welcome me into her family unreservedly; that I would make it, finally, to my mother's fabled Golden Temple, and that here I would hear from the mouth of a devout and knowledge-able Sikh man, all the wise and true things I've learned today.

I have so much to take home with me and think about. But I am not just reconciled to my heritage now, I am embracing it. I speak Punjabi, I wear a sari or *salwar kameez*, I have my own copy of the Guru Granth Sahib to read. I don't need my family here to do these things, I can do them on my own. I have put away the pain that prevented me before. I feel I can take all that is good from here back home with me to England; yet be glad too that I was born there, that I can call the freedom that country has given me my own.

As for my father and my mother, I realised earlier on this trip that I hadn't, after all, forgiven them. What they did to me was wrong. As Dr Mitra said back in Delhi, they made a choice in going to the UK, and they had other choices once they got there. I didn't need to be forced into a marriage with someone from outside the country I was born in, who spoke a different language to the one I did, who had a different culture from the one I had grown up with and inevitably absorbed. There was no possible justification for that: cultural, religious, or otherwise. My instincts were right, and I'm glad I listened to them and made the decisions I did, hard though my life has sometimes been because of them.

If I still haven't forgiven my parents, I can at least say that at some level I understand them, however unacceptable what they did was. Seeing Kang Sabhu and now this place has brought home to me the power of the culture they left behind. Was my mother dreaming of this, these chants and crowds and candles and myriad points of light around this rippling pool and gleamingly reflected temple, as she paced up and down our front room in Dale Road on cold English winter's mornings, sprinkling her holy water around her from a plastic bottle? Surely she was. Had she had any choice about the shape of her own life? Not really. She had been a teenager herself when she was presented with the husband of her dead sister to marry.

When Mum was dying and I tried to explain to her why I had to leave Jassey, my first husband, I said, 'I don't love him, Mum. I've tried and tried to, but I don't.' My mother raised her frail, sick body off the pillows, turned her face away from me, and spat out, with all the contempt she could muster, the single word, 'Love!' I'm sure she loved her children, in her way, but perhaps the only other love she truly had in her heart was for her religion, for Sikhism, for her one God.

The system that imposed her destiny on her was one that had worked for generations and could have gone on working well, perhaps, with our generation too, had we all stayed out here in rural Punjab. Being offered a husband from a nearby village, with a farm of their own, as Bachanu was Gurdial, was maybe a recipe for a happy and fulfilled life. You had your family round you, your relatives nearby, you worked hard on the land, this was how it had always been. But trying to keep that system going thousands of miles away, in a culture so different, which you had never even fully accepted as your own, was bound to create problems.

My mother and father clung on to what they knew because, as Dr Mitra said, they didn't want to fail, they wanted to do the right thing by their lights. But they did fail, didn't they? They failed their children and ultimately they failed themselves.

They weren't alone. Right across the UK, others were struggling to impose the same alien rules. It wasn't easy, and they were forced to draw on whatever they could to help them: a distorted concept of their religion, the support of their equally misguided peers and community leaders, outright deceit to their own family members. In many places the struggle goes on, against the odds, creating weirder and weirder hypocrisies and hybrids of thought. Would Guru Nanak have sanctioned the unhappy lives my sisters were forced to lead? I don't think so. Would he have allowed the abuse of their husbands, brought from India as adults to a land allegedly paved with gold; or the double standards of the next generation, who talk in one breath of 'white meat' and in another of 'pure Asian girls'? I can only imagine what he and the other nine gurus would have made of the perverse, caste-based *gurdwaras* of Derby, Bradford and elsewhere in the West, when this temple they built and defended over the centuries against invading marauders has its four doors to welcome each of the four main castes. In the words of the fifth Guru, Arjan Dev: 'Kshatriyas, Brahmins, Sudras and Vaisyas are equal partners in divine instruction.'

The fireworks fade from the sky. The full moon of Guru Nanak's birthday shines huge and brilliant over the Pool of Nectar. Out against the rippling shimmer of reflected golden light, a lone turbaned Sikh sits astride, what looks, in dark silhouette, like a surfboard with a bucket on one end, paddling slowly from left to right in front of the Harmandir Sahib. I have no idea who he is, or what he is doing, but for me he seems to symbolise the holiness and mystery and serene power at the centre of this vast, devotional crowd.

I am going home now, and am taking all this beauty and power with me. I feel recharged. I have so much work to do.

EPILOGUE

Back home in England again, a few weeks later, my whole journey to India felt surreal, almost like a dream. Did we drive up the GT road? Did we find Kang Sabhu? Did that day with my sister ever really happen? I have the photographs to prove it, so it must have done.

I unwrapped the Guru Granth Sahib from its shiny silver and turquoise wrapping, and the eight chunky volumes stood by my desk waiting to be looked into and studied and read. But that long day we spent at the Golden Temple hardly seemed believable either.

I found myself wondering whether it was like this for my mother, when she came back loaded with all those brightly-coloured clothes and sparkling jewels and shiny plates and exotic jars of pickle. Did the memory fade along with the smell of India, until all she was left with was the plastic bottles of holy water, to remind her, like Cinderella and her slipper, that she had ever been anywhere near the mystical serenity of the Golden Temple?

I had my sister Bachanu's address on a scrap of paper in my in-tray, but I couldn't quite bring myself to write to her. Every now and then I picked it up, looked at it, and put it back down again. It was almost as if a part of me thought that she never had given me that wonderful welcome or that she'd only done it because I surprised her. Perhaps when she stopped to think about it all she would change her mind? And what would happen when my sister Ginda went out there? Would Bachanu stand up for me then, as she'd said she would? I almost needed my sister to have been and gone, and then to hear that Bachanu took my side, for me to believe that the acceptance remained intact. Crazy, isn't it? Yet that's what I couldn't help but feel.

Meanwhile things were moving forward here at home. My children were thrilled that the journey had gone so well. Natasha in particular was so happy that I was, in part at any rate, reconciled to my heritage. The big Asian wedding she's looking forward to is a year and a half away, but it's already starting to shape up.

A couple of weekends after I got back we had the formal engagement meeting at Anup's parents' house, to meet the extended family and discuss the engagement party. In true Asian fashion, this was just the preamble, the event proper isn't until next August. That will be a big ceremony, in a hired hall, with perhaps three hundred people present. From my side there'll be just me and my children, but that can't be helped. Anup's family have been more than welcoming.

To lend me some support at this meeting I asked my nephew Ranjit whether he'd like to come and represent our side of the family, and I'm happy to say he agreed. He brought his wife Balla, and they came along with the four of us: Natasha, Anna, Jordan and me. It was great for me because I was able to say, 'Here's a nephew from my side of the family.'

Even with this preliminary gathering there are still traditions to be followed about which I know very little. When we rang the bell, and Neelam opened the front door, she poured oil on both sides of the step before I walked in. 'What do I do now?' I was thinking, half-wishing one of my sisters was there to tell me. But I greeted her and Anup's father as normal and that seemed to be all I needed to do.

The hallway and the rooms beyond were packed. There were relatives on both Anup's mother's and father's side, everyone standing waiting with smiles on their faces.

'Sat sri akal.'

'Sat sri akal. Sat sri akal. Sat sri akal. Sat sri akal.' People had travelled from all over, up from London and elsewhere in the UK. It reminded me of being young and our front room being full of our extended family. Once we were all gathered, one of Anup's dad's relatives went round the room and introduced everyone, starting with his grandfather and going down through the generations to the children.

There comes a point where the women go and sit in one room and the men in another. So Gugsy went off with Anup, to drink alcohol and watch football and do male things, and I stayed behind with Natasha and Balla and the aunties. I had a lovely conversation with Anup's mum, Neelam, and was able to thank her properly for the loan of all the Indian outfits.

Me and my sister.

'I pretty much gave up wearing Western clothes by the end.'

'They're so much more comfortable in that climate, aren't they?'

'By the end they almost felt like a second skin.'

Neelam was so thrilled, she said, that I had got such good use out of them and that the trip had worked out so well.

'Natasha tells me that your sister may even be coming over for the wedding.'

'Yes,' I said, and in that moment I have a wonderful vision of Bachanu surrounded by all these different ages of Anup's relatives gathered here in the room today.

'We're so happy to have Natasha in our family,' Neelam said in a quiet moment a little later. 'She is such a lovely girl.'

'We feel the same way about Anup. Sometimes I feel like I lost a Sunny and I gained a Sunny.'

I was wearing Western clothes that day, but then so were many of the others present. I've lost my hang-ups about saris and *salwar kameez*. After India I feel quite relaxed about Asian dress. If I want to wear it for a particular occasion, I'll wear it. And when Neelam and I go out to India as we plan, to buy Natasha's wedding sari, I'll definitely be back in those comfortable Eastern outfits.

Another development that's come out of the trip is perhaps more significant. I've decided to change my name. I'm going to take my father's Kang back. Having seen the name in the *patwari*'s book, with my father Chanan and my grandfather Bichu and my great-grandfather Dila's names all attached to it, I feel that I would like my children to carry it on. So I'll keep Jasvinder Sanghera as a pen name, but in my private life I'm going to be Jasvinder Kaur Kang. I'm going to take my father's surname with pride.

For Christmas I put together a little photo album for Natasha. She had so wanted to come along on my journey, and it was my fault that she didn't, so I wanted to make it up to her. I printed out all the photographs we had taken from the moment we got on the plane at Heathrow. I wrote, *Natasha, I know how much you wanted to come, but this wasn't the journey for us to do together, even though you were there in spirit for me every day. That journey comes later – next year!*

And then one day in the New Year, out of the blue, early in the morning as I was leaving the house to catch a train to an event, I got a phone call from India. It was Bachanu. Her loud Punjabi voice rang out down the line. 'I was worried you'd forgotten about us all,' she said, cheerful as ever.

'Of course I haven't forgotten about you.'

'So when are you coming to see us?'

'We're hoping to be out later this year.'

'With the children I hope?'

'Yes.'

'Good. How are they all?'

'They're fine.'

'And Anup and Tony too?'

'Yes.'

Then she wanted to know all about the wedding and how that was progressing. So I told her we have now at least planned the engagement party and I've met all Anup's family.

'Your sister Ginda is coming to see me soon.'

'I know she is.' I paused, not wanting to spoil this first proper communication between us since my return to the UK. But then I couldn't help myself. 'So will you be telling her I visited you?' I asked.

'Yes I will! Why would I not tell her something like that?'

I had to laugh as I was reminded of my sister's sense of humour and energy. 'Well, let me know what she says.'

'I will. I hope you and I will be speaking again soon.'

'We certainly will be,' I said.

'Don't forget we're all coming over for the wedding.'

'Oh, I won't.'

It was only a five-minute call, but it gave me such energy. How is it, I thought, as I sat on the train, that the sister born and raised in India takes me into her life with such warmth, yet not one of my siblings raised here in England would ever do such a thing? It's a big question, but I'm going to have to let it go. A new healing has started within me since returning from India. Part of that is the fact that I overcame my fear and went. Part of it is that I now feel completely comfortable with my heritage. But part of it, too, is that I really have let my English family go. I have no fight left in me for them.

I went back to Derby again the other day. A friend from the city had been staying with me up in Yorkshire and I was taking her back before driving Jordan on to see his grandparents in Nottingham. After we'd dropped my friend off, on a whim, I decided to make a little detour.

'Where are we going?' Jordan asked, as we headed up past the pleasant detached houses of Warwick Avenue.

'I just want to show you something,' I said.

We drove up into the light industrial area around Ascot Drive.

'This is where your grandfather used to have an allotment,' I told my son. 'I used to come up here with him pretty much every Saturday morning and help him plant vegetables.'

It's years and years since I've been anywhere near the allotment, and I was half-expecting that the whole thing might have been built over or developed. But it was exactly the same. The big rusty iron gate was still there, unchanged. Luckily there was someone in there and it wasn't locked, so we were able to drive in and park the car exactly where Dad would have parked it.

'I used to shut this gate for him,' I told my son, 'and swing on it too. It seemed a lot bigger when I was a child.'

Dad's little plot was still there. The shed has gone and the new owner has put up a greenhouse in its place, with potted plants on shelves and a spreading tomato plant at one end. But the tap where we used to put our hosepipe was still there.

'When I was out in India,' I said, 'I saw the piece of land that your grandfather used to farm before he came over here to England. It was like this only twenty times bigger, so it would have been lots more work. They didn't have running water in those days either. He would have had to carry all the water he needed from the well in a pot. It's hot out there, so that would have been hard, backwards and forwards under the sun.'

Jordan was wide-eyed; because he doesn't have an extended family he loves all this family stuff.

We walked round the greenhouse and I looked down at the soil, the very same soil Dad and I used to work all those years ago. 'When we'd done our day's digging and planting,' I said, 'I used to sit here with your granddad. He had an old deckchair that he kept in his shed. He'd put it out here and sit sipping his tea from a flask. Sometimes he'd have a bit of whisky too. He kept a bottle in the shed.'

'What would you be doing, Mum?'

'I'd have been running up and down, messing about, probably. Then I'd stop and sit here and your grandfather would tell me stories of India. Now that I've been there I can see it. When Dad was putting his fingers in this soil he was really putting them in that field back in India. There was a beautiful shady tree at one end of the plot that he used to sit with his friends under in the evening, drinking and talking. A *peeple* tree is what they call it. I'm going to take you and your sisters out there next year, so you can see it for yourselves.

'Are you really?'

'Yes, I am.'

There was a little silence. I imagined Jordan was sitting there thinking about his trip to India. But: 'D'you think Grandfather ever wanted to go back?' he asked.

'I expect he probably did. Some of the time. But he'd come over here by then, hadn't he? He had made a long journey and brought his family with him, so he couldn't just up sticks as easily as that.'

'So why did he come in the first place?'

'When you see Kang Sabhu you'll understand that. It's a beautiful place, but there's not a lot of opportunity there. It was a hard life and they were poor. Your grandfather was ambitious, he wanted things to be better for us all. So he came over here where there was work and money and prospects for his children. He was a brave man, your grandfather.'

Myself and my daughters at the Inspirational Women Awards.

Ben, Jordan, Anna, me and Natasha celebrating the book launch of
Daughters of Shame.

ACKNOWLEDGEMENTS

A big thanks with love and respect to my children, whose support and encouragement has enabled me to become a whole person, and in particular to Natasha, who being the eldest was there at the begining of my journey and became my best friend in the darkest hours. I didn't realise at fifteen that my decision was for you all, but I know that now, and your independence and happiness lift my heart every day.

My thanks to Mark McCrum, Anup Manota and Tony Hutchinson who shared every step of my journey with me. I thank you, Tony, for friendship and laughs and also for being an incredible emotional support, not to mention a big protective measure! Anup, we are so blessed to have you in our lives (it is no coincidence that you are now Sunny to me). I thank you and your family for embracing us and enabling me to understand a new concept of a loving Asian family. Mark, I thank you for bringing my story to life and for your patience, guidance and support throughout.

My continuing thanks go also to my close friends, especially Trish, a special person who in the absence of family has offered me unconditional love and lifelong support. My love and admiration for you is immense. You have taught me so much and I pray that you will always be in my life.

A special thank you to the BBC, especially Dan Farthing, whose research for the trip enabled me to find my sister. Dan, thank you for being sensitive at all stages of my journey, with its many twists and turns!

Last but never least, thanks to Mark Lucas and Rupert Lancaster, who believed in me from the start. I thank you both for your guidance and for being such a calming influence on me; you are both truly inspirational and have managed to turn a storm into a beautiful sunset. I thank you for the past few years and pray that you remain in my life in the future, as you have become part of my new family.

I would also like to thank Anne Cryer, MP, for raising the issues relating to honour-based violence and forced marriage. She has often walked the road less travelled by MPs – and not with any thanks, either. Anne, your contribution to this cause has helped and continues to help so many. I pray that others follow your lead. Thanks also to Vernon Coaker, MP, who has always been willing to listen even when it meant me bombarding him with emails, visits and calls seeking help. Your intervention saved our helpline and I thank you for bothering to make enough noise to effect real change. This is the true job of a politician.

Thanks and respect also to every human being whose family has made them feel less than worthy for taking a stand against wrongs. You are worth more than you know and they have a duty to love and protect you and stop making excuses. I acknowledge you and your right to say 'no' and live a happy, peaceful life beyond disownment.

Praise and thanks go finally to God. My faith restores and keeps me, every single day. Amen.

APPENDIX: KNOWN VICTIMS OF HONOUR KILLINGS IN THE UK

1995   Taslem Begum, 20, Bradford. Run over three times and killed by a motorcycle driven by her husband's brother after she refused to apply for a visa for her arranged husband to join her in the UK and started a relationship with another man.

1999   Rukhsana Naz, 19, Derby. Six months' pregnant when her mother sat on her legs while her brother strangled her to death with a skipping rope. Rukhsana refused to abort the baby she'd been carrying, which her family suspected was not the child of the man she'd been forced to marry at 15.

2000   Jaspal Sohal, London. Wanted to leave her arranged marriage and was battered to death by her husband with a hammer.

2001   Nuziat Khan, South London. Found strangled after she asked her husband Iqbal Zafar for a divorce. He fled to Pakistan. He was suspected of the crime by her family, the police and others, but never returned to face trial.

2002   Heshu Yones, 16, Acton, West London. Stabbed 11 times by her father Abdalla Yones, a Kurdish Muslim, because she was 'too Westernised', had started a relationship with a Christian boy and planned to run away from home.

2003   Anita Gindha, 22, Manor Park, London. Ran away to Wolverhampton to marry the man she loved and escape an arranged marriage with a man from India. Strangled while eight and a half months' pregnant in front of her nineteen-month-old son.

2004   Arash Ghorbani-Zarin, 19, Oxford. Stabbed 46 times by the brothers of the young woman who was carrying his baby, Marina Begum, with whom he had planned to spend his life.

2005   Navjeet Sidhu, 27, London. Unhappy in her arranged marriage. Killed herself and her two children aged twenty-three months and five years by jumping under the Heathrow Express at Southall station. Six months later her mother killed herself in the same way at the same place, leaving a note in Punjabi describing her guilt and loss, and regretting arranging her daughter's marriage.

2006   Samaira Nazir, 25. Stabbed eighteen times by her brother and cousin, before they cut her throat, witnessed by her two daughters aged two and four. She wanted to marry for love, an Afghan man from a different caste.

2006   Banaz Mahmod, 20, strangled by hired killers at the behest of her father and uncle after she left a violent husband she had been forced to marry to start a relationship with a man of her choice.

2006   Uzma Rahan, 32, Cheadle Hulme, Manchester. Beaten to death with a rounders bat by husband Rahan Arshad, after she was discovered having an affair. At the same time he also killed their three children, Adam, 11, Abbas, 8, and Henna, 6.

2007   Surjit Kaur Athwal, 27, Hayes, West London. Worked as a customs officer at Heathrow. Lured to Punjab for 'a family wedding' in 1998 and disappeared, after her husband discovered she was having an affair. Husband Sukhdave and mother-in-law Bachan finally convicted of her murder at Old Bailey in May 2007.

2010   Shafilea Ahmed, 17, Warrington, Cheshire. Disappeared in 2003 after refusing a proposed suitor from Pakistan, saying she wanted to train as a lawyer.

Attempted 'suicide' by drinking bleach while in Pakistan. Her badly decomposed body was found hidden by the river Kent in Cumbria in 2004. Several members of her family were arrested, most recently in September 2010, after allegations from Shafilea's sister Alisha that they were involved in the murder. All were subsequently released on bail, and the case remains unsolved.